The Part
I Remember

The Part
I Remember

CHARLES F. WATERMAN

ILLUSTRATIONS BY J. M. ROEVER

Winchester Press

To my wife Debie, who cooks
the things I write about.

Versions of several of the stories in this collection have appeared previously, as follows: "Clothes," "Old Kelly," "Toby," "Long Distance," and "A Matter of Principle" in the Florida *Times-Union;* "Fly Fishermen" and "The Chum Line" in *Salt Water Sportsman;* "Bluegills" and "The Worm and I" in *Florida Wildlife;* "Waders" and "Grayling" in *Fishing World;* and "Squirrel Dogs" in *Florida Sportsman.*

Copyright © 1974 by Charles F. Waterman
All rights reserved

Library of Congress Catalog Card Number: 74–78701
ISBN: 0-87691-149-1

Published by Winchester Press
460 Park Avenue, New York 10022

Printed in the United States of America

‹‹‹‹‹‹‹‹‹‹‹‹‹‹‹‹‹‹‹‹‹‹‹‹‹Foreword

Though most professional outdoor writers secretly harbor a fine conceit about their own skills, the conventions of the trade demand that they avoid boasting as they would a convention of killer whales. Hence their autobiographical references tend to be stilted, guarded, and downright misleading, and any reasonably objective party of the second part ought to do better.

I'm not sure that I'm all that objective, even though I'm one hundred percent second part. Because frankly, I'm just a mite jealous of ole Charley W., and once or twice, as I read this latest work, my eyes have narrowed and the involuntary thought has arisen that this guy ought to go back to being a professor of English literature instead of making his colleagues in the vineyards of outdoor writing look so bad by comparison. However, if you'll allow for this bias, I'll be happy to give you a party-of-the-second-part look at Waterman.

Let's examine him. He's average-sized and middle-aged, a typical muscular farmhand. He drinks mild potions of bourbon instead of a civilized scotch on the rocks, but is otherwise quite normal. Although the "Waterbucket's" home is in Florida's citrus country, he has no noticeable regional accent, perhaps due to extensive travel and service as a combat cameraman back in the bad old days when we were all winning a war for democracy.

His wife, Debie (always written "Debbie" by name-droppers), can hold her own with rod or gun in any company. She keeps the man honest, articulate—and outfishes him often enough to guarantee humility.

Charley features a patented grin, not jack-o-lantern, but pretty close. He affects cowboy hats and tight denims and roughout boots, but he's equally at ease on a podium in Boston's Back Bay or on a stream bank under the Grand Tetons. The cuss is an accomplished raconteur, a superb after-dinner speaker. Unlike so many of us who write, he is quite as entertaining off the cuff as in print.

Waterman has a wry sense of humor, the ability to say something very quietly—after which you do a mental double-take, and then break up. His approach is completely irreverent and as hilarious as life itself, yet the humor never bites. Charley simply pinpoints the ridiculous, aims shafts at himself, and makes you grin a crooked grin while muttering—*me too!*

Often I think he is a little too sneaky, and this sidebar is added to keep him from getting a swelled head. Constantly he extols the ability of others and downgrades his own skills in the arts associated with hunting, fishing, and natural history. To hear him tell it, he's the inventor of wind knots, inept casts, bumbled leads in wing-shooting, and all of the other little nasties that plague outdoorsmen. But he protests too much. Sure, he throws wind knots and misses game birds. If there are any among us who do not, then I salaam to superman.

The great thing about Cousin Chas is the fact that he has been there and he has done it all. Waterman knows the disciplines: he is at home with plug casting, fly casting, and spinning gear. He knows the mountain torrents and the big seas. He knows how to swing a shotgun and sight a fine rifle. That he also writes like an angel (with a slightly cockeyed halo) is lagniappe.

The Part I Remember covers a lot of territory, and each story is a slice of life guaranteed to please those who have traveled this great country and experienced similar emotions. There is expertise nicely contained, the sensitivity of a sophisticated gentleman who truly loves woods and waters, and the delightful humor that spoofs while it teaches.

Obviously I like the works of Waterman. In a world too often peopled by instant experts, he is a refreshing type who never just looks—he sees!

—Frank Woolner

‹‹‹‹‹‹‹‹‹‹‹‹‹‹‹‹‹‹‹‹‹‹‹‹‹‹‹ Contents

‹‹‹‹‹‹‹‹‹‹‹‹‹‹‹‹‹‹A River Gone

THERE ARE RIVERS THAT HAVE CHANGED or faded because of man and there are rivers of other times that I shall not see again, but there are some rivers that are gone forever.

When a river is dammed there comes a day when the booming rapids become quieter, and within a few hours each one is completely stilled although it has been heard for a thousand years. The riverbed will be there for a long while, winding as it did before, but now on the bottom of a great lake, and the boulders or cliffs that made the eddies and curving runs will now be darker forms in dark depths. If it has been a bass river a new breed of fishermen will probe with depth finders and call the cliffs "structures," and apply the same term to drowned highways and villages.

Much of the James River of southern Missouri has disappeared in a lake that may be of more value than the river was when I first saw it, but because the river is forever gone, the lake has less appeal for me. The dam has been there for only a few years, but I suppose there is already a coating of bottom silt over what was the tricky shoal below Galena.

I caught my first smallmouth a little way above the shoal. I camped with little woodcraft and less equipment in 1928 and I well remember the night noises of an Ozark river canyon—the dull roar of the river itself, the whippoorwills, the owls, the frogs, the tree toads—and just at dusk the musical bay from a hound on some unseen ridge, the distance and direction always vague. There would be a smell of woodsmoke in the canyon on cool evenings, and much of my cooking was done over a log soaked frequently in kerosene. It was much later when I decided camping could be more than a hardship tempering the joys of fishing.

Even then, the johnboats and smallmouth bass fishermen

had been running the river for a long time. The fishermen came from most of the nation's cities, and I was awed that they could afford to hire guides and slide down the river, seated in folding chairs, while a mountain man steered the boat with his paddle and swung it smoothly in the long, slow pools when water was low. A "float trip" could be from half a day to weeks long, going clear down into White River, and the johnboats and equipment returned by rail or truck while the anglers and guides came back to their starting point by car. Float trips still run on a few rivers in spite of the great impoundments.

Some of the guides of the twenties became nationally famous through the writings of city authors. They wore bib overalls and often the dark felt hat of the mountain country, and they sat on burlap bags that contained their spare clothing. They used homemade paddles with which they could pass a flat bottle from boat to boat without a slip, and they could pole upstream if need be, using the handle of a sucker gig. One of them, Charley Barnes, took me catfishing one night when I was about twelve years old. We set trotlines and caught channel catfish and then we gathered some bullfrogs and I asked Charley Barnes if he liked to fish for bass. He grinned in the lantern light and said he hadn't bothered to learn to cast but that he sort of liked to watch the sports do it while he ran the boat. I don't know if he ever did learn to throw a plug. I didn't know then that he was famous, but I read of him many years later.

Our farm was a hundred miles from the James River, but somehow I coaxed my father to take me there several times when we'd finished cultivating corn—and then I would go myself when I should have been working on the farm. My father, who never fished, took me very sadly as if my fishing passion were an incurable disease, and I guess it was.

The best way to fish the river on most occasions was to float it, casting the lures tight against the rocky bluffs or the willowed edges, except in the deep, chunk-rocked pools where a fish might come up from anywhere as a dull brown shadow and then turn to gleaming bronze as it jumped and the rod dipped. When I floated it was usually only an hour or two at a time, and to experience that brief glory I would pole, drag and paddle a heavy johnboat upstream for half a day, wading in the shallow tails of the pools and through the fast stretches where I would hold the boat to the quietest parts and hunt for the dead water below big boulders. Then I'd come back down to my starting point, casting feverishly with my tubular steel rod and anchoring occasionally, placing my Peck's Feather Minnow or my Tom Thumb plug as close to cover as I dared without a disastrous hangup.

But although floating was productive by the hour, it took so much splashy stumbling and so much backbreaking poling and paddling to get upstream that I usually fished from shore or from as far out as I could wade in my sneakers. In June, wet wading was likely to be chilly, especially in early morning and late evening, and only a small fraction of the good water could be reached.

Then there was that late June when weather was very hot. Perhaps it was in search of more oxygen that the bass moved into the faster water. There they were, holding behind boulders and in the foamy eddies along the willows, and I located them by accident during one of my brief floats. There had been time for only a cast or two, and as I went over the shoal (all rapids were "shoals"), the squared nose of the planked johnboat thumping rhythmically on the waves as it found the center of the flow, one fish flashed up from broken water just as the current gathered itself for the descent. I missed that one, but another struck as I shot through the swiftest part of the run, and I knew the fish were in really fast water that day. It was no time for float fishing.

So I beached the boat and waded in at the lower end of the fast water, far enough in so that the current piled against my ribs and shifted the gravel I stood on. I caught bass that struck unseen in the boiling border of the main current, and I had a string of them when the float boat came through. I heard the men's voices raised above the roar of shoal water and then saw the boat coming down, bobbing between the boulders while the guide dug his paddle and the two anglers held their rods still and waited for slower current. I caught a bass only twenty yards ahead of the boat, and the man in the bow, dressed like a city outdoorsman, couldn't believe it.

"Is that a bass, son?" he asked, and I guess I made a show of the heavy stringer as I lifted it.

"We haven't had a strike all day," the second man complained testily, and the boat was past and beginning to slow for the pool far below.

I know now that I must have resented the prosperous floaters, for showing a string of fish has never since given me so much pleasure, and for once the bib-overalled kid in the old straw hat had lived up to what the outdoor artists have claimed for him all these years.

It was a fine day, and as the boat slid into the pool below me, the guide, whom I had never seen before, turned on his gunnysack cushion and gave me a deliberate, unshaven grin. That's the part I remember best.

‹‹‹‹‹‹‹‹‹‹‹‹‹‹‹‹‹‹‹‹‹ Fishhooked

Fish long enough and i guess you can count on getting stuck by a fishhook or, worse yet, sticking somebody else. I had a pretty good record on fishhooks until that day with Ikey House, who used to guide snook fishermen.

Ikey, who doesn't use a fly rod, said nice things about the way I managed to cast without catching the boat or its occupants and I confessed it was only a matter of superior skill. I'd never hurt anyone with a fly or a fly line, I said. Completely unnecessary, I said, if you knew your business.

It was fifteen minutes later that I changed my cast from one side of the boat to the other, and as I crossed over with the line in the air I felt and heard something peculiar. It was a sort of tug and a sort of thwack. It took considerable fortitude to look back, but after a fifteen-second period of oppressive silence, I did.

Ikey was rigidly at the oars, a fixed grin on his face, and there was a neat slice along his cheekbone with a little trickle of blood. Since it was twenty-three miles back to the dock I did not get out and start swimming, but I thought of it.

I knew another guide who wore a construction worker's hard hat when he went with new clients. It was so strong a hint that he had little or no trouble with flying lures.

"School bass fishing" involves schools of black bass which are busting bait on the surface. Although it is fun to rush from break to break on a lake, there is added tension when you anchor on a river at a known "schooling ground" and wait for the fish to come up, never exactly where you expect them, but almost. Three men in a fourteen-foot boat with plugging rods cocked and using multihooked lures can look pretty scary. I knew one otherwise cool character who used to let go all holts

5

when the bass popped and the baitfish showered. I watched him in action from another boat one day. Call him George.

There were two other guys in George's boat, all of them sitting down when that first menhaden skipped, and a five-pound largemouth made crashing sounds hot on his trail. The three fishermen were up and throwing pretty fast, but George, as usual, was first. His big plug went back hard and snagged one of his friends in a place that would have been protected if his friend had remained seated. George didn't look back but yanked violently, his eyes glued to the booming bass.

"Leggo!" he yelled. "I wanna cast!"

One other time on a schooling ground a friend of mine got a hook in his hand and another friend of mine, a cabinetmaker, decided surgery was called for. He whipped open a tackle box, produced a fish knife, honed it to razor edge and stalked the cringing victim who didn't even have a bullet to bite. A third man sat stiffly erect in the boat's bow, his arms folded. Within a few minutes the operation was over and the cabinetmaker beamed with satisfaction.

He turned to the third man in the bow, still rigidly erect with a purplish face.

"Now that was pretty good, wasn't it"—long pause—"Doc?"

And the third man, a prominent surgeon whose qualifications had been forgotten in the emergency, nodded stiffly. It is not ethical to steal patients.

There was this fellow who walked into the emergency ward with his face swathed in amateurish bandages and tape. He'd like a tetanus shot, he said through a small opening.

The doctor on duty gave him the shot and then asked what had happened.

"I got a trout fly in my chin," came the report from the little opening in the bandages, "and my buddy cut it out. He did a lousy job."

"Okay, let's see it," said the doctor.

"Don't touch that tape," came an alarmed voice. "If you move it my whole chin will fall off."

And the patient strode briskly from the hospital. My friend the doctor has worried some about that.

One of the world's famous fishermen is partial to bass bugs, and he was using a big one in a high wind down in Florida when it somehow was whipped against his upper lip, and there it stuck. It was numb for a minute but never did hurt much. However, the Famous Fisherman figured it called for professional skill, and he headed for the nearest town, wearing the gigantic yellow popper like a mustache.

Luck was not with him and the doctor's waiting room was crowded, so the Famous Fisherman entered with his head down, hoping he wouldn't be recognized and wondering if a paper sack with eyeholes would have been a good idea. He saw the rug, a circle of feet, and enough of one chair that he knew it was vacant. He got into it as unobtrusively as possible for a six-foot-two man in chest waders.

His eyes moved across the feet about him but kept returning to a pair of small, bare, muddy ones directly across the waiting room, and he distinctly felt a stare from that direction. An irresistible compulsion forced his eyes slowly upward from the muddy feet, up the blue jeans, and finally to a grave, freckled face, its eyes glued to his. Beneath the nose on the upper lip was a hook, still festooned with an angleworm.

It was then that the Famous Fisherman displayed the aplomb that had helped make him famous, one of the things that separates great men from the rest of us.

"Where did you get yours, son?" he asked.

Business Associate ≫≫≫≫≫≫≫≫≫

T HERE IS A POINT AT WHICH a mature and intelligent hunting dog may begin to replace his instincts with reasoning, and it is such dogs that become legends.

Perhaps there is no thrill to compare to a puppy's first point, but he has stopped and stood because some intangible thing from ancestors long gone has frozen his muscles. When it first happens I wonder what goes through his puppy brain, for he is a sort of innocent observer of the whole thing—probably amazed that this scent has made him rigid when that of a bone has only made him hungry. To the unscientific hunter, if he thinks about it, the instincts of pointing and retrieving are unparalleled examples of heredity, and while training shapes and polishes them, they have been there all along.

But this brings us to the other things, the beginnings of which set a dog apart. There is the retriever who decides without guidance that dead birds must be brought to the particular individual who fired the shot—or perhaps he must decide the downed game should be divided equally among the hunters, no matter how much trouble it becomes. And there is the unprogrammed business of jumping straight up and down to flush a nearby pheasant when the hunter is close by and the bird might otherwise run instead of flying. For the moment a pointer borrows from the flushing breeds.

Then there is the very attitude of pointing, and there are great old bird finders who do their work in very relaxed form, no longer galvanized into classic poses by the magic scent but simply reporting the presence of game because they know it is there and the shooter wants to know.

McGillicuddy, the old Brittany, had all of these perceptive habits, the frivolous business of pointing style having lost its importance long ago—the porcelain point giving way to a

calm indication of where he thought the Huns or sage grouse should be. McGillicuddy would mark a plunging chukar covey until the birds were only specks in a Washington chasm, and if someone had fired and one bird landed short of the rest he'd start the precipitous journey without urging. You could say McGillie knew what was going on.

There was the time when I had no dog and the mallard drake surprised me. He got up from a narrow, deep section of a creek and didn't hang up there the way jumping mallards sometimes do but went off low across a close-grazed stretch of grass on the other side, a nearly bare area fifty yards across and surrounded by brush and timber except where the creek bordered a little of it.

It hadn't seemed I was quite on, but the mallard came down near the center of the opening and lay flat in the grass without moving. I watched it for a couple of minutes and then went upstream to find a shallow crossing place. Of course when I came back to the open spot the mallard was gone, leaving only half a dozen gray feathers. It was a crippled bird, I had been stupid, and now I spent almost an hour probing nearby brush, feeling sure the cripple would be hidden within a few feet of the open ground. The section of creek that bordered the bare ground offered no visible concealment.

So with the self-accusation that always goes with cripples I trudged unhappily back to my car and drove ten miles to town for McGillicuddy. Almost two hours after the duck had fallen I brought him to the half-dozen feathers and tried to explain the situation. McGillie listened attentively, his tongue sticking straight out a quarter of an inch as it always does when there is a knotty problem. He declined to sniff the feathers.

He didn't vacuum the ground as he usually does when someone mentions a dead bird. And he paid no attention to the fifty-yard clearing. Even humans could find a bird there. He trotted briskly around the perimeter, almost all the way, with his head high. Then he stopped still on the creek side, looked straight at me and made an elaborate point toward the creek; then looked at me again. Together we walked to the water's edge. I could see nothing there and the banks were close-cropped. McGillie was eyeing me instead of the water.

Then he trotted upstream to an easy entry spot and came paddling down to near where I stood, turned into the bank and almost disappeared. Only his stub tail and his energetically working hind legs showed. It was an unseen undercut and he finally managed to back out with the duck, so we went back to town, McGillie napping on the back seat.

Of course he had scented the mallard—or had scented its route to the creek, taken nearly two hours before—and figured out the rest.

I put him back in the kennel with courtesy and respect. I don't own McGillicuddy but I wish I did.

But then maybe nobody really owns a personality like that. He's a sort of business associate.

Crazy Quail ›››››››››››››››››››

EVEN WHEN THEY ARE NOT GLARING over a traphouse I am not completely at ease with shotgun champions, for they have something I have not and cannot really understand.

There is the alert relaxation between shots, and if their palms sweat and their knees quiver I cannot see it. Then, there is that moment when the point of concentration is almost visible, sizzling steadily over the traphouse, and one of them calls "Pull!" in such a way that the target is not only commanded to appear but ordered to shatter, all in one word. And when one of them misses I cannot believe it is a human miss but something mechanical such as a defective pattern or a target that is overly hard. Although I speak of trapshooting there is much the same in skeet, simply not so easily observed.

There are hunters who can appease their egos with the statement that target shooters are no good on game, but this is seldom true and it has given me no satisfaction. Then we rigged this Crazy Quail setup.

Now we didn't have the trapshooters in mind at the time. We just wanted to miss fewer birds, and this fiendish pit with the revolving trap seemed a good idea. The good thing about Crazy Quail was that the rules were just suggested and everybody was doing a little extemporizing. You can find these pits around quite a few gun clubs, but a lot of them have fallen into disuse because you can't stop shotgunners from keeping score.

It's just a hole in the ground with a trap rigged on a turntable so that a sadist can sit on a seat and fire clay pigeons at any angle from the ground and in any direction. We fixed ours so you could keep the targets very low except on the side where the victim stands with his shotgun. You have to keep a high shield there for protection of the trap operator. At first we thought it was just for accident prevention, but later we saw its merit as a crime deterrent. By the time a gunner ran around that shield he would have thought better of shooting the trap boy.

Now with our rules you'd call for the target with the gun-stock below your elbow. We had quite a discussion about the distance from shooter to trap, and you must remember that the targets come toward the shooter as well as away from him and our rule was that he couldn't move his feet and take them behind his position. We considered twenty-five yards, but somebody envisioned a rifle-bored trap gun with one of those cold-eyed target smokers taking his time and ruining the whole show.

But we had to place the shooters back some to keep the skeet guns honest, so we settled on sixteen yards. One of the natural features that helped was a stand of oaks and slash pine off to the left. They seemed to swallow any target that went that way—really tough visibility—but Buddy said a swamp quail doesn't carry any taillight either and it would be good practice.

Now if the guy in the pit made mental notes on each shot he'd quickly learn what your tough angles were. If the targets smoked when you hit them he'd figure you had a tightly bored gun and he'd tear you up with close ones. If you took them quickly he'd guess your gun was open and he'd fire most of them nearly straight away at a low angle to get them out of range fast. Then, there's the gimmick of establishing a pattern until the shooter begins to second-guess the trap and he's really psyched.

But the main gimmick of our setup was the juvenile delinquents who began to hang around—some teen-agers who had nothing to unlearn, shot well themselves, and could be happy for days after making a fool of a man with a $2,000 shotgun, preferably a man with straight-run patches on his shooting jacket.

They quickly learned the tricks—the target with a hole

punched in the center so it would drop fast—the daisy-cutter that barely cleared the pit edge—the funny noises that sounded like the trap but weren't.

Anyway, a bunch of good shots came over and got their nerves shaken. There was one who threw his new trap gun on the ground and there was one who slid his Krieghoff into his car and muttered that he not only couldn't hit the damned things but that his match shooting would be ruined for the next weekend.

But the one I remember was the poor soul who studied the setup carefully and had done better than average. He not only had the skeet champion's cool eye but he had the birdshooter's quick and easy swing, and he was bent on ten straight. It looked as if he might be well ahead of the young rascal in the pit. He crouched a little and his left hand held the forend lightly. Now he made one dry run, the polished walnut jumping to his cheek in a flowing move, and then he lowered it and called "Pull!"

There came a nerve-shattering thump as his unseen tormentor kicked the sheet-iron pit wall. He started just a little but smiled tautly and waited. It had been too long, so he called "Pull!" again. And when he saw nothing he called "Pull!" a third time testily, and finally he saw a coal-black, unpainted target disappear in the black shadows beneath the darkest pine.

Then came a muffled, boyish voice from the pit, quivering on the edge of derisive laughter.

"Mister, I done done it twice and you ain't seen it yet!"

«««««««««««««««««««The Salmon

I want you to understand how the place is laid out.

The salmon camp is on a high bluff so you can sit on the porch and watch the best salmon lies along that section of the Mirimachi. The river is split by a long island that lies in front of the camp, but there's no good water on the camp side of the island. When you fish you take a canoe at the foot of the bluff, cross to the island with a dozen paddle strokes, and then walk on across to the salmon water.

When someone is fishing on the far side of the river you can spy on him from the porch with binoculars, and if the wind is right you can hear loud conversation. When fish are in, *most* of the conversation is loud.

On that day things had been pretty quiet and we rested for a while at midday. I was dozing on the porch when a boat came down the river and a man got out with a very small boy, probably three years old. The man waded in on the far side and I could see the sun glint on his line as he laid his fly over the long run. The little boy had some chirpy comments from time to time but he seemed satisfied to watch his dad fish.

I reached for my binoculars when I heard the reel squall and saw the salmon flash in the air. It was a good fish and it smashed back with a white bloom of spray. Within a couple of minutes the fisherman began to follow it downstream, the little guy tagging along and talking a blue streak.

They'd gone about a hundred yards when I saw the fisherman would have a problem and I put my elbows on the porch railing to use the glasses better. At first the fisherman had simply walked along the shelving bank, his line stretching out and downstream, but now he came to a giant boulder projecting into the water and the river bank was almost vertical above it. It was a matter of wading out and down, and the swift pool was no place for a three-year-old.

The man waded out and bent his rod more sharply, but the reel squealed jerkily again and he began to give way downstream. For a few moments the little boy was silent and then he told his daddy not to leave him. His father called not to worry, that he'd be right back, and continued to crab down the heavy run, rod tip high. Then some willows cut him off from my view. Within five minutes the little boy was sobbing his troubles and wailing his fear.

The boy stayed well back from the water but I tried to help calm him anyway. I scooted down our bluff, crossed the near channel in a canoe, hurried over to the other side of the island and made comforting sounds across the main channel, which I couldn't wade. He quieted down temporarily and I hiked down my side, through the willows and past the poison ivy and the spot where the woodchuck lived. Far below at the very downstream tip of the island I could shout across at the fisherman. It had been about an hour since the salmon struck and the angler was showing wear, tear and a little despair.

"I need help," he said. "I'm tired out and this tailer won't work—or maybe I don't know how to work it. The fish came loose."

Hoping he wouldn't take me up, because helping a stranger land a trophy fish is in the category of smoothing over a family fight, I asked if there was anything I could do.

"Anything would help," he grunted. "Is my boy all right?"

The poor guy had a real crisis, so I hurried about a quarter-mile to the canoe, went back to camp, put on my waders and learned somebody else would go over to comfort the little boy. Then I paddled the canoe down to the scene of action. The man had dropped still farther downstream, well below the island, and he'd pretty nearly reached his limit unless we used the canoe. The water was deep and the bank steep. I didn't show my big salmon net at first.

The salmon was about done. It was hanging almost on top

out in the main current in plain sight, its dorsal fin and tail cutting the surface part of the time. It was an old-timer and I could see scars on its side. It held slightly downstream from the fisherman and there was no doubt it could be pulled to shore, however briefly, if he could get below it, but a boulder and deep water barred the way.

He showed me the tailer that hadn't worked for him and told me how tired he was. It was plain he was holding the fish very lightly—too lightly—but after more than an hour there was no way of telling how much of a hole the hook had worn and I respected my long-term rule of keeping advice to myself when somebody else has a fish on.

"Well, what should I do?" he said.

That was when I took the big net from the canoe and he suddenly looked happy, but his face fell when I said I wasn't going to net his fish.

"You can't pull him much farther downstream," I said. "Just work him into shore and at the last second I'll hand you the net."

"No way," he said. "Please, you net him. If you miss there's no harm done because I can't get him by myself."

And I think he said *please* again, so there I was on the edge of deep cold water with my hands beginning to sweat around the net handle and wishing I'd never watched the river from the porch.

Now, I know how to net a fish headfirst as well as you do, but this was a special case and I reasoned that I had a pretty jumpy customer on the rod. Maybe, I thought, I could net the fish from the rear as he hung in the current if he'd just swing in close enough. So I waded in as far as I dared, feeling the shove of current and the lift of deep water on my waders, and I told the man to ease the fish in if he could.

At first the salmon swung his head and resisted the leader's pull but he began to come closer, probably so tired he didn't even know what was happening. The pull was almost at right angles to the current but I was afraid to suggest more downstream pressure for fear the fish would go so far down we couldn't get him back up. Then we'd have to use the canoe and the fish had already been on too long.

And after what seemed a long time the fish was within reach of the net, just a little above me, his fins moving slowly and his angle just a little away from the rod's pull.

In violation of all rules, I eased the net under water and pushed it toward the salmon's tail, dismayed that the current was so forceful against the coarse twine. I wondered if I could move it quickly at all. The big hoop was actually past his tail and inching forward almost to his dorsal fin when the salmon saw it and made a determined though weakened effort at lunging upstream. That was when I heaved forward with the net and there was a great splash, made partly by the salmon and partly by me. Water went into my face and choked me when it entered my stupidly gaping mouth. Cold water went into my waders and for a moment one foot could find no bottom at all.

I lunged backward toward the bank, floundering and over-balanced by my extended arms and net. As I crashed down on solid stone and earth I dragged the net up and out. There was a large salmon in it.

The man stood over me and eyed his prize.

"You know," he said, "you're supposed to net salmon head-first. Always headfirst."

He can go to hell.

‹‹‹‹‹‹‹‹‹‹‹‹‹‹‹‹‹‹‹ Camp Cooks

Despite sentimental flights about the joys of dining with your eyes full of hot ashes, I have found few camp cooks I care to associate with near mealtime.

Sir, if you know a good, practical camp cook I suggest that you foster his friendship at all costs if he is a male; if a female, make every effort to marry her.

My opinions lack some authority because it has been said that I could starve to death locked in a supermarket. A lack of enthusiasm for culinary camp chores has made me a dishwashing expert of many years' standing. From this lowly station I have observed that my wife can serve a Christmas dinner for twelve with fewer dirty dishes than required by my fishing buddy in preparing a quick breakfast for two.

I do not overlook some of the efficient shortcuts employed by male sportsmen. An outstanding example is the system of a pretty fair dry-fly caster I knew who served ham and eggs twice a day, explaining that the enclosed protein and stuff were just what hungry fishermen needed. But it was in economy of effort that he excelled. He served the ham and eggs on plates each morning. Each evening he turned the once-used plates over and you got ham and eggs on the bottoms. It meant a single washing for two meals and a boon to my department, but it required some skill to eat sunny-side-up eggs from a face-down plate, even though he somehow achieved a leathery base from the egg white.

As a dishwasher I have had rare opportunity to witness the inside operation of amateur camp cooks—their triumphs, their dramatic failures, and their moments of gnawing anxiety. They are fundamentally a fidgety and insecure lot. Most of them can hardly find the kitchen at home.

Some years back I was privileged to be appointed dishwasher for a camp of Southern deer hunters. The camp was a spacious cabin on a picturesque lake shore, and it was my choice to be dishwasher since I had no stomach for a turn at cooking for four other guys, all of them admittedly chefs of a high order. I wasn't a regular camp member; only a guest.

When I moved in the day before season opening I wished to make an impression with willingness and announced my first official act would be to clean up the dishes and rearrange odds and ends stored under the sink counter. In the South such hunting camps are frequently carried over through generations, and the odds and ends are evidently inherited too. When I started out it was simply a chore to impress my friends, but as I got on with it I had all the anticipation of an anthropologist digging in Aztec ruins.

Such resorts are furnished mainly with things no longer needed in the owners' homes, so it was not surprising to find twenty-eight water glasses in a camp with beds for six hunters. There were thirty-three coffee cups, some of them marked with the names of deceased marksmen. None of the four broken electric toasters seemed repairable, but the eighty ·assorted knives and forks were okay. *Currently* used dishes and utensils were in a separate cabinet.

In the cooking-grease department, nothing had been wasted. Contained in a variety of cans, old coffeepots and jars was something like five gallons of used grease. The entire inventory was frequently interrupted as the hunters kept moving in to exclaim over some long-forgotten bit of culinary memorabilia and after a brief conference they decided one gallon of secondhand cooking grease would be sufficient.

There was a flurry of excitement when I found an old-fashioned jug of colorless liquid with a unique bouquet. After that treasure had been whisked away the hunters were so interested in sink secrets that I lacked room to work.

Each of the other hunters at that camp took his turn at dinner cooking, usually beginning elaborate preparations around six p.m. Since they contested bitterly with each other as to the

quality of their respective specialties it was generally about ten p.m. before the various ingredients were gathered and the food on the table. The meal was sleepily completed around eleven p.m. and I'd generally get dishes washed and the kitchen cleaned up by midnight. This was rather inconvenient since all alarm clocks were religiously set for four a.m. I'd have ended the week worn and haggard if anyone had gotten up at that time, but we actually crawled out about six a.m. and the carefully planned and elaborate breakfast would take until about eight. We generally started hunting about nine o'clock.

The cook with a specialty isn't purely a product of the South. Almost everywhere I go camping I find a saucepan Caesar who insists on feeding the assemblage something better then they get at home. He presses all hands into service as assistants and gets the meal on the stump about two hours late. He usually lacks one of the most important ingredients and if a market can be reached by an hour's arduous driving he probably runs into town after the Cantonese bead molasses he needs for his beef and noodles. If it's a backpacking expedition I insist that he carry his own groceries and utensils.

When you return from one of these all-male campouts, give your wife some flowers. It will seem the least you can do.

‹‹‹‹‹‹‹‹‹‹‹‹‹‹‹‹‹‹‹‹‹‹‹‹‹ Salty Talk

I HAVE SPENT MUCH OF MY LIFE AFLOAT, but they were very small boats for the most part. My first trailered rig was a cedar skiff that rode precariously on a trailer made from an old buggy, iron tires and all, and I have never owned a yachting cap.

I didn't know how touchy this nautical-speech business was until I wrote a thesis titled "The Sea Language of Herman Melville" and barely passed the course. My observations on Mr. Melville's deepwater rhetoric were very shallow, the instructor said.

Then, when I got into the Navy and found myself an instructor in the Navy school of photography at Pensacola while I was still wearing my white hat round, I had another setback. There were no walls on a Navy station, I learned. There were bulkheads, stanchions, decks, overheads, hatches, ladders and passageways. There were no pillars, floors, ceilings, doors, stairs, or halls, they told me, and I became a salty talker to impress the lads who came in from the fleet to learn the mysteries of photography.

The terminology put me at ease when I went to sea myself but when World War II ended I became something of a backslider, climbed back into canoes and little outboards, forgot how to bend a bowline—and even cast from the floor of the boat occasionally while braced against the side instead of the gunwale.

Since I was engaged in writing about hunting and fishing I frequently made reference to boats and parts of boats and was tactfully reprimanded occasionally by those who specialized in writing about boats, and not so tactfully by owners of new cruisers who had just finished Coast Guard Auxiliary courses.

Inevitably there came the time when I was to have a fishing

skiff built to my specifications and a locally well-known ma-
rine designer flattered me by taking me back into the plant to
discuss final details. I admired the nearly finished sixteen-
footer and really watched my language. There had been that
time when I had written about oarlocks and Jim Martenhoff,
boating editor of the Miami *Herald*, had gently explained to
me that what I meant was "rowlocks," not "oarlocks."

I caught myself just short of asking for "oarlocks" but I
stopped in time.

"I'll want some rowlocks on there if it's not too much
trouble," I said.

"Sure," said the designer, "no problem. Do you want them
in the front end or the back end?"

<<<<<<<<<<<<<<A Time for Snipe

At dawn there had been the sounds of Canada geese preparing to leave the lake to feed, goose conversation that had meanings to practiced hunter ears and carried for great distance in the damp half-light. The carefully placed decoys looked real in the open field then—in broad daylight they would turn to fakes easily classified at close range.

When the calls became more urgent and changed their tone we knew the Canadas were leaving the water and would cross near us, and although we did not expect them to decoy with set wings and groping paddle feet we hoped some little band would turn in uncertainly, change their calls, and glide briefly at reasonable range. We waited for this in our brush blind, yawning nervously and feeling our familiar gunstocks for reassurance. Only one little group came near that morning, but we killed a single goose and then waited for another hour since not all of the birds had left the lake. It was early autumn and not very chilly, even there in Alberta near the Alaska Highway's beginning.

While we waited and the sun made a bright spot in the low clouds a rag-tag flight of small birds passed the blind, going like inept flight students and as if their leadership were in doubt, making high-pitched and raspy noises, seemingly irritable complaints about their sketchy flight plan. When I announced they were jacksnipe my Canadian friend stared after the erratic specks and confessed he'd never even noticed them before. There were many snipe that day, but somehow it was not a time for snipe shooting although an obscure paragraph in the game laws indicated open season.

Two months later in Montana I carried a rucksack of mallard decoys from another blind, my waders breaking annoyingly through a frozen crust over sticky bottom, and trudged along a creek below a dam where a trickle of a leak left a path of soft mud fringed by gleaming ice. A snipe twisted away over the willows with his harsh *"scaip"* (some believe he says, "Escape!") and several more left at intervals in typical snipe nonconformity, evidently feeling the first was an alarmist and stubbornly insisting on their own judgment about when to flush. Between there and the truck I watched twenty more snipe leave. They had been there the previous day but before that there had been no snipe at all. The shotgun was open-bored, for I had been shooting decoyed ducks that plunged downward from the level of cottonwood crowns, and the uncomfortable lump in my camouflaged jacket was a handful of skeet loads for the snipe I knew would be there, but I did no shooting. Both the snipe and I were heading south, some of them from the Arctic Circle, and somehow it was not the time or place for a snipe shoot.

In January I stopped the skiff's motor as it nosed in to shore and then I poled it through a gap in the dark cypress knees, shoving hard to penetrate the tiny cove's mat of hyacinths, the boat making a scrubbing sound as it moved grudgingly. Ahead was a wide grassy flat bordering a slough that entered the river under a hyacinth carpet. There were only a few scattered trees on the flat, but there were some clumps of switchgrass as much as three feet tall. Most of the flat was short coastal Bermuda grass, less than six inches high, and a quarter-mile away on the inland side were the blotches of Brahman cattle willing to graze with their feet in water. Near them were the tiny white specks of cattle egrets and farther back were oaks waving Spanish moss.

At the slough's border was a great blue heron that moved off for only a short flight as I waded through the rim of cypress that bordered the river, and on the grass were clusters of white herons, egrets and a band of white ibis. Killdeers were everywhere, and when I caught the sunlight just right I could see the gleam of water through the grass, that little film of wetness which means a probing beak could find worms beneath it.

Some of the large wading birds flew away from me but would not leave the flat entirely, and it was a quiet place except for their calls. The shells seemed to click loudly when I dropped them into the little double's chambers, and it was a time to enjoy the firm snap when the breech closed.

I turned downwind so that a flushing snipe would swing into it and show his light underside rather than scooting away unseen for the important first ten yards. The first one went up off to my right and had made his squeaky call before I saw him, too late. On the short grass they watched me long before I sighted them, and I tried vainly to get a clump of switchgrass between me and a bird so that I could work closer than the twenty yards at which they preferred to jump. It did not work. I watched a bird leave and then realized he had been within range, so I missed the next one at much too great a distance. There were flocks of a dozen or more that went up together, dissatisfied individuals peeling away on their own course at intervals, and there were single birds that went up until they were specks, circled for a mile or two and came back to the spot they had originally left. But they were wild snipe and only one made the turn to inspect me at close range, seeing a frustrated and sweating gunner in hipboots who somehow missed just as the bird completed his observation and turned away.

There were a few of the plungers who change to arrowheads somewhere up there and hurtle downward as if prepared to pierce the earth's crust, check their dives at the last instant, and land gently with an overdone nonchalance. The snipe did all of these things as they always do for lonely walkers on the bog, gunners who are a little out of step and go hunting specifically for snipe, whereas most snipe shooters are raucous fellows who are merely taking a little time out from slow duck hunting and are carrying fours or sixes in addition to the number nines they brought for the incidental snipe. At other times these pagans might be woodcock or grouse gunners with reverence and love for their game, but I feel they regard snipe too much as mere targets and care little where the birds were hatched or where they roosted last night. They make jokes about shooting snipe over a barricade of empty shell boxes, but they leave the Wilson snipe with little dignity. I may have been like that myself when snipe season first opened after a long closing of many years ago.

On that day in Florida I worked farther and farther from my boat and I resolved as I have resolved many times to take only those birds that arose immediately in front of me and to ignore derisive cheeps from the side or back. It was a warm day and the boots became heavy. The gun was light but my arms ached from carrying it at the ready, the checkering making a pattern on my damp palms. My eyes smarted slightly from unrelieved staring at the grass ahead, and in the back of my mind was a dread of checking my empty shells against my bag when I got back to the boat.

I felt that the big wading birds which refused to leave the slough had a jeering tone to their calls and that the plentiful robins and occasional yellowlegs were stationed in the cover to confuse a snipe hunter. But the game and I were at home and I hardly heard a boat on the river and cars on a distant highway. It was a time for snipe hunting.

‹‹‹‹‹‹‹‹‹‹‹‹‹A Hunter's Ghost

I DO NOT BELIEVE I REALLY saw a ghost. A symbol, perhaps, but not a ghost. I did not want to follow it or study it too much for fear there would be a simple explanation, and I did not want an explanation of it, nor do I want one now. I want it left just the way it was.

We were in northern California and it was shortly after World War II. Our expedition was pleasant but not glamorous. We had been on a varmint hunt with pistols and we left from some hilly ranch country before dawn to drive back down the coast to San Francisco. Fog had closed in solidly and there was only a gradual transition between dark and daylight, so I was driving with the lights on at about the time dawn should have been.

I do not recall having met another car on the road and I could have been going no more than twenty-five miles an hour, hoping for a break in the gray monochrome that held visibility to thirty or forty yards. There was barbed wire on both sides of the road and it was foothill country, not extremely steep—grazing land.

The first hound appeared against the fog on the road shoulder, larger than life somehow because it was there as if projected on a screen with no reference for size, a great dark fellow moving at a lope to cross the road, and I braked instantly as he passed. If he or the two immediately behind him saw or heard the car they gave no sign, and they had almost reached the fence when the man appeared on the same course, moving somehow at what seemed an incredible half-run, half-walk, swift and silent, and the fog revealed the upper part of him before his legs and feet as if he were floating above the ground. He seemed neither to see nor hear the car and crossed very close ahead, a rawboned giant in a broad-brimmed, slouched felt hat, and I am vague about his clothing. Was it all gray or was that an effect of the fog? I think it was only shirt and pants; no coat. He had a long gray beard and long hair and in those days, many years after one fashion for beards and many years before a new style, he had a wild look as if he had followed his great hounds forever and would follow them forever more. He stared straight along the route the dogs had taken and seemed to step over the highway fence with hardly a break in stride, but I am sure he simply pushed the top strand down and crossed without waste motion.

His rifle must have been a long-barreled Winchester '73; at least the outline was the same, and I know that the bluing was worn so that it was the color of bare metal.

He was plainly outlined against the fog and then gone completely and I had heard nothing. The car windows were up and there had been no trace of the hounds' baying although they must have been trailing. When I turned off the engine and rolled down the car windows I heard nothing and it felt as if the world were fenced by cotton batting. The sun came out a little later.

I like to think he still follows his hounds on an endless trail he has kept since his rifle was new. There is probably a prosaic explanation of him and his dogs but I'd rather not hear it.

ᐊᐊᐊᐊᐊᐊᐊᐊᐊᐊᐊᐊᐊᐊ Gun Collecting

I HAD A BROKEN CIVIL WAR MUSKET when I was very small, something that had belonged to my grandfather, and I persuaded my father to cut it off with a hacksaw so it would be more convenient to play with—and finally it found its way to the junkpile against the stone fence back of the chickenhouse.

Then as a teen-aged trapper I found an older muzzleloader in an abandoned barn, masked by cobwebs and standing in a dark corner with a broken pitchfork, the sort of discovery gun collectors dream of but seldom make any more. In depression times gun collecting seemed a frivolous pastime, and I sold that prize for fifty cents to a young fellow learned in firearms matters. He said he'd study up about it and decide whether to junk it or not but I believe now that his hands shook a little as he handled it.

Years later when the old home farm was sold I went back and looked for the 12-gauge Hopkins & Allen singleshot my father had used for rabbits and the crows that sometimes raided our newly hatched Rhode Island Reds. Its stock had been bolted together because Dad once broke it over an opossum's head. He'd heard a midnight ruckus in the chickenhouse and had missed a quick shot at an indistinct shadow, but when a pair of gleaming eyes came toward him in the lantern light before he could reload he smashed the invader with the stock. That was the gun which had kicked me off my muddy feet when I first fired it at a sitting duck. But it had disappeared from the old home place and I never found it.

So after a lifetime of wanting and having guns I found the other day that I had no antiques—or even near-antiques. There is some sentiment in the Colt Official Police .38 with which I once won a minor pistol match. It has the old King ventilated rib and the cockeyed hammer installed by the great Bob

Chow for timed and rapid fire. The trigger pull still goes like breaking glass and the grip shows honest wear—but it would never mean anything to anyone else.

I wish I knew what became of the .45–70 trapdoor Springfield with which I missed the coyote, and I wish I still had the Belgian hammer twelve with the side latch and the graceful straight grip I didn't appreciate when I was thirteen.

This old Parker had been around and it was out of place among new guns in the little hardware store. The breech was tight but the rust had been there for a long time and one firing pin was broken. It could be repaired, of course, but that would be expensive. Get $35 for it, the owner had said when he left it with his friend the hardware dealer.

So I bought it for $35. No, I told the dealer, I didn't need to know where it came from. I took it home and rubbed off some of the worst rust and smeared a little Linspeed on the dry surface of the stock, bringing a dull glow to the smooth parts and to the deep scratches.

I don't know if it was a pot hunter's gun or if it belonged to a man who swung it quick and smooth and swept back both hammers together in a single click as the barrels came up. But

I like to think it was there when the dawns were cold, the decoys chuckled over the eelgrass, and the cattails swished in the north wind. Possibly it pointed across the prairie grass when the wild chickens rose in skeins up ahead and the wagon creaked behind the gunners.

I hope the pointers floated ahead of it, testing the brushy edges and checking the palmetto patches near where the bobwhites had dusted. And plover may have wheeled above it, sparkling as they caught the sun.

When I brought it into the house my wife looked at me a little strangely and must have silently recalled my scorn for "guns I can't shoot." But she mail-ordered some little hooks to hang it with and we put it on a paneled wall in a place where it doesn't show much except on sunny days. It could be seen better in several other spots, she said, but I don't care if anyone else sees it as long as I know where it is.

It has to take the place of the old muzzleloaders, the Hopkins & Allen singleshot, and the .45–70. I am not much of a gun collector.

The Worm and I ⤜⤜⤜⤜⤜⤜⤜⤜⤜⤜⤜

I WOULD RATHER NOT FISH with plastic worms. Oh, I'll do it if there's no other kind of bass fishing to be had, but I am not screaming and scratching to get to the worm counter.

Since some of my best friends build plastic worms for a living and since other friends fish with virtually nothing else, this soul talk may take me off some Christmas lists, but it is time I stood up and was counted.

I am not competing with the danged things. More than ten years ago I learned that, under most circumstances, the skilled worm worker can get up later and catch more fish than I do with plugs or flies. I am a little ashamed of my old friend the black bass when he actually refuses to let go of a worm, even though the hook isn't stuck in him, and I have turned my head away sadly when I have seen a yearling bass actually jump on a tight line, hanging to the hookless tail of a spotted plastic worm. Even when he finds there is a 200-pound man on the other end, a half-pound bass is willing to fight for a thing he doesn't recognize and never saw before in his life. It is almost as if they built the bass to go with the worms.

It may sound like an unfair crack at what's probably the world's most deadly black-bass artificial, but I have watched a number of worm fishermen reach an hour of decision. There seems to come a time in the life of every worm fisherman when he has it down pat and figures there's little more to learn. As I see it, he has three choices:

He can continue fishing worms with increasing skill and bask in the admiration of ordinary fishing mortals for the rest of his days while catching a devil of a lot of bass.

He can decide he's mastered the worm phase and look around for a kind of fishing that can now be a new challenge.

He can give up fishing.

Plastic worms have not been kind to me. There was the time when a lady sat in one end of a boat and caught and released twenty-six bass on plastic worms, and I caught one in the other end. Her husband, who did the rowing, said I needn't feel badly, that she was a pretty good worm fisherman.

There was the time when I anchored on a bass schooling ground on Florida's St. Johns River and caught two bass with my plugs while a guy anchored fifty feet away simply worked plastic worms along the bottom and caught about thirty, turning them loose. He described his fishing in a sort of play-by-play monologue and I think that was what irritated me. I find that any other fisherman who is catching more fish tends to be just a little insulting.

Whenever two or more worm fishermen get together they generally start talking about what a plastic worm represents. If it's in lizard country it represents a lizard, they say, and if it's in big-worm country they say it represents a worm (that's not startling), and if there are quite a few snakes around they say it represents a snake.

Somehow the word is out that a black bass loves to grab a snake at every opportunity, and I had begun to subscribe to that idea until I was watching Walt Dineen, a fisheries biologist, opening some bass a while back. Dineen found something that was partly digested and at first wasn't sure what it was but finally figured it was a snake. He said that in the thousands of bass he'd inspected he'd found less than a dozen with snakes on the inside. Well, there goes that bass "fact."

"What," I asked, "does a bass think he's getting when he takes a worm?"

"Just something easy," said Walt. "He's never seen anything like it before but it looks easy to catch and easy to swallow so he grabs it."

If biologists are going to keep coming up with undramatic explanations like that, how are we perceptive, colorful and fascinating fishing writers going to retain dignity in our professions? Fortunately, most worm fishermen don't care what a bass thinks it is as long as he wants to eat it, and perhaps the bass thinks it's a plastic worm and good to eat. Some of them *are* good to eat, you know, and some small boys buy the licorice-flavored ones for that purpose. A friend of mine has two kids who are hooked on plastic worms and he keeps them under tight rein when he enters a tackle store. However, don't go around munching all kinds of plastic fishing lures. For all I know, some of them may be deadly poisons. Anyway, if you have to lunch on a lure, be sure there's no hook.

«««««««««««« Fly Fishermen

I HAVE OBSERVED FLY FISHERMEN for forty-four years and report herewith in the interests of research. Most of the names
have been changed to protect the guilty.

By illustration, Jeff is running for Congress and it would be
a political stab in the back to use his real name: no true saltwater fly fisherman would vote for him after learning he uses
an automatic reel; the fact he is a fly fisherman would lose him
the spin fishermen votes; and the nonfishing public would turn
away after learning he fritters away his time angling. See?

There is nothing wrong with an automatic reel in many sit-
uations and it has considerable merit when fishing the south
Florida canals, which is where Jeff uses it, but I think his is a
prototype for the first commercial model. He can take it apart
in the dark and frequently does, and even when it is running
perfectly, its takeup sounds like a beach buggy stuck in scrap
iron.

Jeff and I were fishing on the Florida Keys and, fishy-smell-
ing and stained with salt water, we dropped into what we
thought was a scruffy lunchroom for a hamburger. In the Keys
you should be more careful than we were because some of the
fancier places disguise themselves, and this was one. Busy lying to each other about fishing, we were seated in the center
of the crowded dining room, wet pants and all, before I saw
we were in the wrong place and an upswept French-type
waitress with a little white apron had handed us menus the
size of the table.

Jeff, who has the kind of voice a Congressional candidate
needs, supported by an unusual accent, never glanced at the
menu but ordered a can of 3-in-1 oil, and the waitress, who
had big eyes anyway, scampered back to the kitchen for a conference. They'd probably already heard Jeff's order back

there, because there had been dead silence from all the other patrons since we'd entered. Now there was a discreet scuffling of chairs as everybody shifted to see us better and Jeff whipped out his original automatic fly reel, pushed back the orchid centerpiece, and dismantled the thing on the table-cloth with the dexterity of a shell-game expert.

The only hitch was that the spring somehow tossed a small part to the floor and Jeff pursued it on hands and wet knees under a nearby table where he recovered it among a forest of nylons. He and the waitress got back to our table at the same time and she regretted there was no reel oil in the place, a sur-prise to Jeff, who said in pear-shaped tones that it was very unusual. He could have been heard on nearby U.S. 1.

He announced to the world that he would repair his reel without oil and proceeded to do so while everybody's seafood got cold. I do not recall what we ate, but restaurant-wise things were almost back to normal when Jeff finished the job and touched the lever for a trial run.

The old clunker howled, "Whuzzeeeee—Whap!"

Somebody dropped a dish of Key lime pie and there was a tinkle of falling silverware. I went outside and I guess Jeff paid the bill. He said the reel was fine again.

Florida canals are a good location for a study of fly casters, and when you fish the roadsides you have to watch your back-cast as it is easy to flip a leader around a convertible from Newark or a semitrailer from Tampa. After years of practice you learn to throw a backcast through the traffic or above it.

I misjudged some time back when the snook were hitting small bait against the opposite bank and the wind made a low backcast advisable. I saw this station wagon coming at about sixty-five miles an hour, towing an outboard boat with motor attached. I decided on the spur of the moment that I could let the car by but my backcast could be tossed over the boat. I never thought about the possibility of adverse air currents and one of them sucked my line down and wrapped it around the motor. I've lost many a fly through similar errors and snapped leaders, but that was the first time I got the *line* hung. There was about 150 yards of strong backing and I was unable to slow the station wagon.

In fact, I was unable to let go of the line that was paying through my hand, and if anyone tells you any fish goes as fast as a station wagon towing a boat he's a damned liar. The reel thawed pretty badly and my hands were in bandages for a while. Anyway, I threw the rod and reel onto the ground and jumped on them so the backing broke off at the spool.

If you happen to have that line, I can identify it. It is a white, weight-forward No. 10 and there is a little blood on the running part.

I have learned a lot from canal fishermen, part of it by direct confrontation and part by peering through gaps in the sawgrass.

When I was fishing beside a fellow we'll call Rocky, I noted that he was catching roughly eighteen fish to my one although the snook were blasting wildly just across the narrow ditch. I asked him why and he said I had to throw the fly clear into the grass on the opposite side and pull it out past the fish, which he said were facing the grass and herding the bait against it. I did and started catching fish same as he did.

Next day I came back to the same spot and started in confidently, but I couldn't catch anything while Rocky was cleaning up again. Again I inquired.

"Hell, man, you gotta change things now," Rocky said. "The fish are facing this way today."

Science.

Fly fishermen are primarily men of strong character and firm allegiance. I was fishing for largemouth bass with a fellow we'll call Cuthbert. His favorite fly was a frightening streamer he called the Purple People Eater. We were standing on a canal bank and the small bass were thick but Cuthbert wasn't doing too well. I'd caught eight fish on a popping bug and as far as I could tell he hadn't had a bump on his pet dingus.

Finally, he caught a single undersized bass and ran over to show it to me.

"Man," he said, "that old Purple People Eater sure gets 'em. Do you want to borrow one?"

Faith.

Another guy whom I shall call Ted Smallwood has special fishing methods. To make it interesting we'll pretend he owns a fishing resort on the southwest Florida coast.

He and I and a fine fly caster I'll call Buddy Nordmann ran an outboard boat for twenty-some miles to a place Ted said the snook were tearing it up in a mangrove creek. When we got there the winds had changed the tide and water was so high it was impossible to cast back under the mangrove bushes where snook live.

I rowed and Buddy cast beautifully from the bow. Ted, who was in the stern, announced he would fish a little, too, although he didn't care about it, and since he didn't have his rod he would borrow the one I had been using. Since it was a sleek little 8½-footer belonging to my wife and Ted doesn't exactly employ a feather touch in salt water I had some misgivings, but there wasn't much I could say.

Flipping his fly like a master, Buddy hadn't raised a fish but Ted started catching them right away. He'd slam the streamer into the bushes and then yank it away with a lot of swamp-rat rhetoric, shaking the whole loosely attached shoreline. At first I thought he was just dumb and awkward but I finally realized the snook were coming out to see what was going on and would clobber Ted's fly. He was about as stupid as a shot-stung pintail drake.

I was about to tell Buddy what was going on when the boat slid over a network of sunken logs some twelve inches under the surface. As we passed them Ted made a series of hangup jerks in the mangroves and a big snook rose silently from the depths of the log jam about seven feet from the boat and gave us a cold, delinquent stare. Ted dapped his streamer near the fish's nose and it disappeared in his mouth, whereupon Ted set the hook violently in what I figured was an impossible situation. But again the swamp fox thought he knew what he was doing.

Ted, who looks like an over-age Rams tackle, just lifted up on my wife's rod and hung on. His huge forearms bulged and the sweat ran down his nose. The leader tested twelve pounds and the whole snook weighed fourteen but I don't know what his front ten inches would weigh, and that's the part Ted held out of the water until the snook gave up. The rod made funny cracking sounds but it never gave way. I dropped both oars over the side. After Ted released the fourteen-pounder we went back to the dock.

My wife said there was something wrong with her rod.

"It must be softening up," she said. "It needs a lighter line."

So she gave it away and got a new one.

An experienced fly caster can throw a reasonably good line with a hoe handle but he invariably decides on a particular type of rod which he swears is better than anything else. Possibly it is a very short, stiff one and possibly it is a long, soft one that requires a tall fisherman to prevent the tip from dragging the ground.

Generally the accepted test of a fly rod is how far you can cast with it. This is equivalent to judging a new sedan solely by its maximum top speed, but fly fishermen are not ordinary people.

Now there was the salesman we'll call Hubert. He sold all kinds of fly rods but he was hooked on one type—stiff as a poker and about the same length. He could do a good job with it and carried on a perpetual demonstration on the lawn, in supermarket lots, and at various fishing camps. Though this rod had definite advantages it was not a distance stick, an obvious fact Hubert refused to recognize despite all sorts of concrete proof. Such earnestness in fly fishermen is sometimes confused with pigheadedness.

Now one day Hubert wheeled his car up to a crowded fishing resort and staged a demonstration before a group of people who were interested in fly fishing, and since I happened to be present and had known him for a long time, Hubert invited me to try some of his rods.

Several models were already strung up and I chose a medium-action nine-footer that would throw a line farther than Hubert's pet with no effort whatever. I took some pleasure in doing this, knowing all the time that Hubert could do the same thing if he'd lay down his freak stick and pick up a more standard rod. The audience viewed Hubert as if he had just washed ashore and walked back to their cottages.

But the next day he was back and somehow got a crowd of prospective customers together again. He then rounded me up and invited me to do some more casting with him. Figuring this cluck was a born patsy and maybe just a little stubborn, I consented and when Hubert unlimbered his wading-staff type of rod I simply reached into his car and took out the same stick I'd used the day before.

Hubert laid out a fair length of line on the grass and, without moving it and in an unnecessarily loud voice, challenged me to equal it.

I tried but nothing happened. Overnight the creep had substituted a peewee level trout line for the big saltwater taper the rod had carried the day before. I looked about me but saw no sympathy in any face, so I walked away leaving Hubert lecturing on the merit of his stub stick.

Crafty.

I went fishing with a fellow who said he thought he needed a new fly outfit. It was getting to be too much work, he said. Maybe he was just getting too old for fly fishing, he said, but he had trouble keeping his backcast up and wasn't getting sufficient distance.

We had a good spot to work for some rolling tarpon, so I slid the anchor over and got ready to cast from a stationary boat. My friend, whom we'll call Jack, was ready first. Just as I was about to work out some line I hit the deck because of an eerie noise that apparently came from nowhere.

The sound was a sort of whistling whirr, a somewhat higher pitch than that of a low-level aircraft, but somehow mechanical and a bit unearthly.

I looked up at Jack but he was placidly watching his bug. It would bear watching.

Although Jack wasn't so much as twitching his rod tip his bug was leaping out of the water, buzzing about the surface and throwing little geysers. It went "Putty, putty, putty," and it went "Ploop, ploop, ploop!" and it gradually slowed to an occasional convulsion and lay still.

Jack picked it up and again came the whistling whirr over our heads, again came the cast and again the bug went "Putty, putty, putty" and "Ploop, ploop, ploop!"

"What in God's name is that?" I quavered.

Jack didn't answer for a minute because a small tarpon sizzled around the thing at high speed. He rolled wildly, bulged under the bug, splashed his tail on the surface, and came to a quick halt, breathing hard, about three feet from the bug. The bug then gave one last ploop, flipped a few drops of water, quivered, and lay still. The little tarpon spun around and darted up a tidal creek, leaving a distinct wake.

"Well," said Jack, "this bug is run by rubber bands. When I make my backcast the wings wind up and the bands get tight. Then when I throw it on the water the bug works all by itself. But it is kind of hard to cast, and maybe that is my trouble."

I asked him if he had caught anything with it.

"Well, no," Jack said, "but it sure makes the fish act funny."

Dr. Clutch was a real whiz on largemouth bass and he never talked a great deal about his methods, some of which were almost clinical in their approach.

Smitty ran a fishing tackle store and a doggoned good one. He was a fine fisherman and a careful student of method, passing on helpful facts to appreciative customers. When Dr.

Clutch came in and told Smitty the bass were hitting and he needed company on an impromptu fishing trip, Smitty was eager to leave the store to the hired help and get with it. Smitty figured he might learn something.

It was a bit sudden, so Smitty left the store in his blue suit with his fly rod under one arm and a plastic box full of streamers and popping bugs in his fist. It was to be a wading trip and since Smitty didn't have his usual waders at the store he grabbed a new pair of chest-highs out of stock.

The doctor had his mind on fishing and drove pretty fast with a sense of urgency. He loaded Smitty into his outboard boat and took off across the flats with the kicker singing the blues and hitting about every other chop.

Now the doctor's system of fishing for bass was to locate a nice patch of grass and go booming up to it in the boat. When a short distance away he'd cut the throttle and the skiff would squat, pushing a big wake into the grass. The wave would stir up the hiding baitfish and some of them would dart out into the open, whereupon the bass would start swatting them. The doctor would by then be out of the anchored boat and laying a streamer fly among the busy fish. Good stunt, but he didn't explain it to Smitty.

Well, Doc zeroed in on a lush patch of grass while Smitty was sorting out his improvised tackle. The boat whizzed up to the right distance and Doc chopped the engine and bailed out in his waders with his fly rod in his hand in three feet of water.

Smitty is not stupid, figured the boat had caught fire and got out too—in his blue suit with his new waders under his arm.

Not everything is known about fly fishermen. As the researchers say, further study is indicated.

Old Kelly ≫≫≫≫≫≫≫≫≫≫≫≫≫≫≫≫≫≫≫

I ONA, S.D.—I HAVE NOT BEEN NOTED for sentimentality and Walt Disney's best efforts concerning the animal kingdom have not caused me to blubber, but my bifocals steamed up a little today—over a speckled dog.

He's getting to be an old dog now and he never has had the nobility of Lassie or the classic pointing stance of Gunsmoke. He's just been an honest old bird dog and although there have been a lot better, none ever tried harder and there never was a more agreeable associate.

Today he loped down a sun-baked South Dakota hill where a hot, dry wind was bending the prairie grass. In the bottom of the draw was a little brush where a game bird might find shade at midday, and down there old Kelly, the Brittany, slowed a little, wiggled his stub tail and then pointed, his tongue lolling almost to the ground.

When I walked up, some brown birds almost as large as pheasants came out with guttural cackling and I shot one, then wonder of wonders, managed to get another before they swept over a shoulder of the draw. Kelly ran over to one bird, nosed it and then lay down beside it, completely tuckered out.

It was just another kind of bird to Kelly but it was the last bird on a long list I'd made up several years ago when I decided I'd try to kill all kinds of the upland game birds of North America over the same dog. Some of them hadn't come easy, like the Mearns quail Kelly pointed in Arizona when only three of his legs were working. He'd been so crippled up after that day in the desert we'd taken him to the veterinary and feared he'd never again use four legs—but as usual old Kelly came through and was on the job six months later.

And the time in Alaska when he went over the cliff after the hard-hit ptarmigan. And the time he rammed the stick into his eye in British Columbia (he never did watch where he was going).

Now, shooting all of the upland birds of North America is not high adventure. Anyone could do it if he were persistent enough, and any dog could point them all if he were reasonably adaptable and someone put him in the right place. I got the idea because I was going to write some stuff about upland hunting and figured the best way to learn about it was to do it.

Now I'll give you my list. There may be some readers who won't quite agree that this is all of the birds, but except for subspecies and slight variations this list was the best I could make. And the bird that old Kelly lay down beside today was the true prairie chicken, a pretty appropriate bird to finish out with because it's one of the most unusual characters of the upland classification and is fighting a tough battle to make a living as civilization continues to trim the grazing lands.

The list of birds goes like this:

Bobwhite quail, Mearns quail, valley quail, scaled quail, Gambel's quail, mountain quail, woodcock, sharptail grouse, ruffed grouse, blue grouse and Franklin's grouse, sage grouse, Hungarian partridge, chukar partridge, ptarmigan, pheasant, snipe, and prairie chicken. That makes eighteen. There are other upland birds not too often hunted with dogs. We got some of those too.

I get tired of hearing men brag about their dogs, and I won't bore you any longer with this. I'm going to get old Kelly off my left foot, where he's taking a nap. Then I am going to put this old portable on the bed in this little South Dakota motel and I'm going out and buy my dog a steak—well, some hamburger anyway.

The above was written several years ago, shortly before old Kelly left us forever. The hills and hedges haven't been quite the same since.

Squirrel Dogs ➤➤➤➤➤➤➤➤➤➤➤➤➤➤➤

GREAT DANES AND CHIHUAHUAS make good squirrel dogs, but bloodhounds don't. Thoroughly mixed breeds are probably best of all—although I didn't realize this until I discussed it with a real connoisseur.

"Look," the expert explained, "anybody who has a litter of registered pups knows they're worth money. Somebody'll keep all of them even if they can't find their own dish. Now you take a mixed-breed pup. He starts life with two strikes on him. He's gotta prove himself or nobody's gonna feed him. If he doesn't think it out he won't last very long."

You follow this through logically and it makes sense. The farther the pup is from purebred stock, the smarter the pup is, because he comes from a long line of mutts that made it on their own with no help from a pedigree.

Now that's selective breeding at its best, isn't it? I was a little embarrassed that I hadn't thought of this angle before.

But, even so, some purebred stock is used on squirrels for lack of anything else. About the worst is a bloodhound. I suggested bloodhounds to an old squirrel hunter I know. Everybody knows a bloodhound has a cold nose and can follow a track that has been rained in.

"Boy," I said. "I'll bet a good old bloodhound would find every squirrel in the swamp and then tree so loud you could stay home and watch TV until he was ready for you."

He said I didn't understand the principle of the thing at all, and he explained by telling me about Old Nosey, a bloodhound used to round up escaped convicts, find lost children, and locate people who were behind with their notes at the bank. You show Old Nosey a sock and he'll find the foot that belongs in it if it takes all summer.

It seems that some fellow robbed a bank and got away with

the president's stuffed bass, so they were more than commonly anxious to lay hands on him. They knew who he was but he had left home, so they showed one of his socks to Old Nosey and Old Nosey took one whiff and was off and yodeling. He trailed the fellow through a pretty big city but the chase ended up at an airport where Old Nosey ran out on the runway and stared off toward Omaha. It looked as if that crook had really made it.

The cops pretty well gave up but Old Nosey was never very happy after that and it was always hard to keep him from running off down side streets in a strange town—and you never knew when he'd stop and bay on a street corner.

He was getting pretty old and had begun to act strangely, but he'd been such a good dog that his owner kept him around. Well sir, one day Old Nosey put up an awful racket as his boss was driving past a cemetery. Thinking the old fellow wasn't feeling well, the boss let him out for some fresh air and Old Nosey went over and barked treed at a tombstone.

It belonged to the guy who had robbed the bank, all right. He'd been dead for a couple of years.

So, you see, a bloodhound is a very poor squirrel dog. Just imagine yourself looking into a tree for a Tennessee squirrel that might have left years ago and gone to Georgia or Alabama.

Another problem with purebred squirrel dogs is that they are apt to have a different set of ideals. A good squirrel dog shouldn't bother about sportsmanship. He should let his boss handle that end.

For example, I used to own a Brittany pointing spaniel named Kelly. His business was hunting birds but his hobby was hunting squirrels in our yard, and the squirrels got right into the spirit of the thing. Almost any day you could look out and see a gray squirrel hanging head down on a tree trunk and addressing Kelly, saying unfair things about his AKC registration and his field-trial ancestors. Kelly would pretend he was asleep on his box.

Kelly would wait until he saw a squirrel a good way from a tree and then he'd let out a yip and take after him, closing in just as the squirrel barely made it. Then the squirrel would turn around halfway up the tree and say a bunch of unkind things about all dogs in general and Kelly in particular.

I was watching one day when old Kelly spotted a squirrel a long way from his tree and accidentally cut him off. There he was, face to face with the squirrel, standing dead still with the squirrel looking first at Kelly and then at the tree.

This had never happened before.

Kelly thought about it for a little while and then backed up about ten feet. The squirrel sat still but hunched down just a little. I don't know which of them gave the signal, but all of a sudden the squirrel scratched off in a shower of leaves and Kelly snarled like a turpentined panther and barely missed him at the tree.

"Why you flop-eared, splay-footed . . .!" said the squirrel.

"Come down here, you fuzzy-tailed barn rat and I'll . . .!" said Kelly.

The point is that Kelly let his breeding stand in his way. As a squirrel hunter he was always an amateur with an amateur's ethics.

It might be I never would have learned anything about squirrel dogs if I hadn't taken up squirrel calling many years ago. There are all kinds of squirrel calls, you know, but this one looked like a sort of artistic type. It was a striker and a little box, and I figured you could say all sorts of squirrel things with it if you practiced a little. There are a lot of squirrels living around our house, which was built on an old oak hammock, and I have listened to them a lot.

One old he-squirrel will stomp out on a limb and say "Chrrk, chrrk" at another squirrel and the other one will say "Kook, kook" back at him. Then they'll jump at each other and squeal a couple of times and one of them will shag off for the tall timber while the other one sits up on his hunkers and looks around to see if anybody else is hunting for trouble.

So I figured that if you could make some of that fight talk

you'd get plenty of attention and big fat squirrels would come out from everywhere to be shot at. It was pretty obvious that our squirrels bragged about how tough they were, so I decided I'd try my call on a big old character we called Tuffy. He had part of an ear gone and all the other squirrels gave him plenty of room when he spoke up.

I waited until Tuffy was sitting by a window raiding the bird feeder and then I tried my call. Tuffy jumped straight up into the air with his feet churning and disappeared into a tree. There were pieces of bark falling for twenty seconds. I never saw him again. I'd give anything to know what I said to him, but in any event I decided I'd better use a dog instead of a call.

A good squirrel dog goes along ahead of you through the forest and when he jumps a squirrel he chases it up a tree and barks until you get there. You take a smart-aleck, self-centered squirrel dog and he'll just sit down and watch when you come up—but a squirrel dog that's worth his bones will help you when you try to get a shot.

You look up the tree and can't see anything of that squirrel except possibly a little fringe of his tail, so you try to slip around the tree to the other side and get a crack at him. He moves. No soap. You throw a stick on the other side of the tree and bruise your jaw yanking your gun up to shoot when he comes around on your side, but the squirrel knows the difference between a stick and a hunter and doesn't move.

Now, rat terriers have a lot of advantages as squirrel dogs, but this is the point where I want a Great Dane. You just motion your Dane over to you and put your hunting coat on him (obviously it would be too big for a Pekinese) and you tell your dog to stroll around on the other side of the tree. The squirrel sees your coat walking around over there and moves around to where if you miss him it's your own fault. With a little practice the dog can learn to clear his throat the way you do, and if you haven't learned to bark like a Great Dane, you just aren't taking squirrel hunting seriously.

A good squirrel dog knows when to keep quiet as well as

when to woof. If none of the aforementioned strategies get you a shot you have to get a little sneaky. Throw a stick as far as you can heave it and have your dog go after it without an audible command. Maybe the squirrel will hear him going off through the dry leaves and figure the coast is clear. Or, you can order your dog to go home and listen as his footsteps fade in the distance, then watch for the squirrel to stick his head out.

There is another system that is pretty advanced but which should work well. After spending quite a while trying to get a shot at a treed squirrel, you can use what I call the absentee approach.

You look at your watch and say to your dog:

"My gosh, it's five-thirty. We can't get home until after dinnertime, even if we start right now. I'm tired of this foolishness. No squirrel is worth missing a meal. Let's get out of this place."

You say this in a loud voice and then walk away with your dog. When you get about seventy-five yards away you stop and tie your dog to a tree and give him your sandwich so he won't make any noise. Then you sneak back toward the tree and wait for the squirrel to come out and laugh at you.

Think, man, think.

⋘⋘⋘ A Matter of Principle

I WAS ABOUT FIFTEEN YEARS old and I was sitting in this duck blind, made up mainly of cattails. There weren't many ducks flying and I hadn't busted a cap. It was a brushy shoreline on a weedy lake, and since I'd crawled in there before daylight I had no idea how many hunters were near me or just where they were located. I did know there were a few decoys set out maybe fifty yards away.

I was almost ready to give up when the bunch of teal put on the brakes up high and I could hear their wings hiss as they came down to look at the lake. They made one circle against the rainy sky; then they set their wings and headed straight for the decoys bobbing just outside the cattails. But before they had killed their speed and while they were still well out, somebody shot one of them and the rest of the flock flew apart like a grenade and whizzed back into the clouds.

A man put forth in a tiny duckboat and picked up the single bird on the water, and it was then I realized he had killed it while it was coming into another hunter's decoys. The man who owned the decoys called to him, just loud enough to be heard—no bluster, just a statement.

"Mister," he said, "when these duck quit flying I'll meet you right back of this brush and I'll beat hell out of you."

"I'll be there," said the other guy from his boat, "but don't come if you don't know how to fight."

I stood in the edge of the cattails and willows. I wasn't hiding but they paid no attention to me. They were big men who had never seen each other before. They seemed older to me then, but they must have been in their late twenties.

They took off their raingear and their coats and began to fight—two big-shouldered men in a little clearing with a mist of rain falling, fighting silently except for the chunk of their

53

punches and their heavy breathing, and occasionally a little grunt. It was bloody and it was businesslike and it went on for quite a while, and finally one of them was down and could not get up. The other man helped him and they put on their slickers, picked up their guns, and walked off in different directions.

They had been gone for several minutes before I walked out into the little clearing. The grass was crushed down over an area perhaps fifteen feet across. They hadn't moved around much. It had been real all right, because there was a little spatter of blood over the place they had fought.

They hadn't been completely quiet, for they'd said something about the duck and I remember one of them took it with him when he left. But for the life of me I can't remember whether it was the man with the decoys or the man who had shot it. The truth is that once they had taken off their rain jackets I wasn't quite sure which was which.

It's kind of fuzzy but I sure can't forget it.

‹‹‹‹‹‹‹‹‹‹‹‹‹‹‹‹‹‹‹‹‹ Turkey Roost

I T RAINED CONSTANTLY AS IT HAD rained most of the day before, coming steadily with little wind—a cold rain that would
total three inches before it was through. It filled the swampy
basins and gradually wetted the back roads that had been
dried to sugary sand.

There had been the moment of real discomfort at three that
morning—the rain muted but insistent on the heavy roof of the
hunting lodge, once a ranch house and seemingly built for all
time. There was only a little longer to stay in the warm bed
and the wry question—*What am I doing here?* The same question comes momentarily before taking a night watch on a foreign sea. Then there was the cheerful breakfast and the drive
through brimming ruts, the little four-wheel-drive jerking its
headlight beams from gleaming palmettos to dripping Spanish
moss, to black oak trunks and cypress knees.

When we stopped and the headlights went out it was a long
moment before the night sky could be separated from the ir-
regular black bank of treetops. No hint of dawn yet and the
guide, Quet (pronounced *Queet*), had me load my gun, for
there would be no clicking or clacking from then on. The
beam of his small flashlight was partly covered by his fingers as
he handed me a camouflaged aluminum stool and moved
away, a bulky simian form in hooded raingear. At first he directed a spear of the flashlight beam near his gleaming rubber
boots, giving glimpses of wet grass, sticks, acorns and puddles
on the forest floor, but he soon turned it off and I followed the
faint outline of his head and shoulders. At a little more than
arm's length he blended into the forest night and I found myself almost in a ridiculous lockstep as I crowded closer. He
made his way unerringly without stumble or hesitation.

We stopped by an oak trunk and used a shred of the light again while Quet cut half a dozen palmetto fronds to build his sketchy blind. He placed the aluminum stools with care and seated himself a little behind and to my left—guide, coach and sentinel. The rustlings of preparation stopped and the sounds of rain were plain again. I had yet to kill my first turkey but the setting was familiar.

I had sat in a clump of palmettos through a spring dawn and heard a gobbler from a cypress strand, and another somewhere in the palmettos near me, and I had fearfully used my call—only a few tentative yelps for I knew I was inadequate with it—and then clutched my gun, sweating with nervousness, to await birds that never appeared.

In fall I had sat back to back with a really good caller and heard the yelps of invisible turkeys a scant thirty yards away in thick swamp—but the sounds had faded and we were left listening to busy gray squirrels and flickers. And there were other times.

I thought dully of those other turkey hunts as I stared straight ahead in the pre-dawn rain, a little sleepy, lulled by the steady mutter of the downpour and hypnotized by the vague pattern of light and shadow before me. There was a great swamp there, I knew. I could make out the taller trees and between the swamp and our stand was a lighter area which I knew was a hyacinth-choked stream. We were on what passes for a ridge in Florida, sloping gently up from the stream fifty yards away.

Quet, the guide, had "roosted" the turkeys the evening before, that woodsman's process of sighting and following from feeding area to roost—a combination of watching, trailing, hiding and listening. His task made harder by the rain, he had seen some birds fly up into the swamp trees although it was more difficult than usual to hear the battering of heavy wings that has given away so many roosting spots.

"I've got some on a limb," Quet had said.

The flock would fly back across the stream for the day's

feeding. In the rain it might be nine o'clock, he thought, but he was less sure of the time than the other factors.

"We don't roost too many turkeys in rain like this," he said. "I don't know when they'll come down."

But we were at the logical landing point; of that he was certain.

Dawn began to seep through the swamp before us and the tallest tree over there became a real tree with branches instead of an uncertain outline. It was fifty yards to the creek's edge, I estimated. It was forty yards to a black log a little to my left—and I went on to other range estimates in case the birds arrived, and I suddenly realized it was light enough to shoot.

It was an old over-under duck gun I held across my lap, the muzzle tipped down a little and just inside our little palmetto fence. The grip was a familiar assurance, the once-crisp checkering rounded with wear and abuse, and I suddenly wondered how it would feel if I needed to shoot quickly with wet hands and a slippery stock. I tightened my fist firmly and felt the scar where the stock had struck a rock years before and I checked the safety to be sure it moved smoothly, but I did not take my eyes off the swamp. We had not moved for more than an hour.

There had been an imaginary bug against my cheek inside my rain hood and a real bug on my upper lip, but I had left them alone. A squirrel came down our big tree and inspected us from five feet away but left without comment.

I did not see the first turkey fly down, hard as I watched, but I heard one land somewhere and I heard the calling as the flock began its day so I knew there were many of them. They can come from the trees swiftly, faster than a quail, and only if you are very near can you hear the hiss of their speed. It is part glide but the great wings often work too and they might go half a mile on the morning fly-down.

I saw several birds in the air, some passing at a distance,

black as giant cormorants in the rain, and then some landed at our left somewhere and yelped only a little.

Quet leaned near enough to whisper against my ear.

"Don't shoot the first one. There's a big gobbler behind it."

And I saw the smaller turkey walking slowly and alertly on a course that would cross a clearing ahead of us at about thirty-five yards, its neck and head above a little fringe of weeds, and I felt calm again, almost sure that now I would kill a turkey although I had the ridiculous thought that the old 12-gauge might misfire. It never had.

And that is the part I remember best—the young tom moving gracefully in the rain against his background of hyacinth-filled water and the deep cypress swamp back of that, all framed in wet Spanish moss hanging from the oaks over our heads. A moment later the big gobbler showed head and neck so I brought the muzzle up slowly and killed my first turkey. But until we reached my gobbler in an open grassy area I do not recall ever seeing any part of him except his head and neck where the shot went.

Wild Sheep »»»»»»»»»»»»»»»»

I DIDN'T KNOW THE MOUNTAIN was so quiet until after I shot the big Stone ram. As I felt the recoil I heard the bullet strike and then the rifle report bounced about the rims and canyons. The ram slid headfirst down from the narrow path he had been racing on, the sun glinting from his heavy horns, and when he stopped sliding he was at the upper edge of a steeper drop-off. A few small pebbles had been dislodged and they rattled a little after the ram's form was still. It was then I noticed how quiet the mountain was.

The wind had died out and it was almost noon. We had climbed for the ram since early morning, first on horseback and then afoot, and until the ram stopped sliding he had been crowding my mind, a growing obsession that would have seemed silly to me three weeks before. Trophy sheep hunters, I had thought, tend to be a little crazy, but when I had lived with sheep hunters and listened to them for a week I began to feel the fever and the push toward the high pastures, almost like the unhappy, overpowering thrust toward the front in wartime. In a week the measurements of record ram horns were suddenly important—figures I had dismissed before as trivial.

Blair MacDougall, the guide, stood over the black ram for a moment before he began to cape it out, an awkward task on the slope. It was a record sheep, he said, and he had the bemused look of a man who has ended a long task and is looking back upon his efforts. He had seen the ram the day before from miles off, studying it with his spotting scope through the dancing curtain of mirage—but it had been so far away he could tell only that the horn bases were heavy and the body large.

And although he had known that particular ram for less

than twenty-four hours it was the climax of the search that began at base camp days before—or was it several weeks ago
when he had come in by bush plane from the Alaska Highway
to round up the horses for another fall?

We cached the meat in a subalpine snow patch, for without
the necessity of keeping concealed MacDougall felt he could
work a packhorse close to the site next day. When he had
lashed the head to his pack frame and I had gathered up the
spotting scope and my rifle I looked down the mountain with
my binoculars and saw a bull moose at the edge of a draw that
must have held a swampy spot. The antlers caught my attention first, flashing white in afternoon sun.

Then I was able to locate our camp, half a day off and far
below, white dots of nylon and a raveling of blue smoke from
the cook tent. Before we came down from the high ridge we
saw a glint to the east, and with the spotting scope were surprised we could make out the village of Trutch, days away on
the Alaska Highway, its white buildings vague blobs dancing
in mirage. To the west were the repetitive snowy peaks ex-
tending to the Pacific, and I thought that this was a far country and very big.

The very presence of insignificant Trutch somehow made
the country more vast, and I thought about sheep hunters—
real sheep hunters. I have tried to do better, but my best as-
sessment of them is concerned with their age, and I brazenly
quote myself from a book called *The Hunter's World:*

"Forty is the finest age of the sheep hunter. In his twenties
and thirties he chases sheep, pursues them in the knowledge
that the ram which eludes him today will have a bigger head
next year.

"But at forty he begins to plan around his physical strength.
Still able to scale the slopes, although more slowly, he now
feels more sharply the beauty of the high places and recog-
nizes that he cannot have it forever. In his fifties he looks up at
the far peaks, smells his camp's wood fire and thinks long of
the tilted grass slopes and the thread trails of sheep hooves on

the high, clean ridges. He knows that though these pleasures may still be savored they are now to be rationed and his quota dwindles as the years advance."

Hunting the wild sheep is expensive, and the older the hunter the more time he must have to reach the high ridges and the grassy pockets with the tiny snow creeks. There is only a little sheep hunting for most of us.

A few years after the big ram fell I stopped at Trutch on the Alaska Highway, but already the place no longer seemed quite familiar. I looked eagerly to the west and saw the seemingly endless mountains and the high spines that faded into progressively deeper haze. Hurrying a little because the sun was almost down, I found a place to hold the binoculars steady and studied the distant ridges carefully to find exactly where the big ram had lived.

But I couldn't be sure. It was just miles of receding ridges and I gave up when the lights went on in the Trutch lunchroom.

Duck Blinds ≫≫≫≫≫≫≫≫≫≫≫≫≫≫≫

Long before dawn the traffic lights blinked for us alone in our small town. Our tires crunched against dry snow on the pavement and a single mongrel dog trotted under a street light, pursuing his route at a slight angle. Our windshield wipers grated against some icy streaks not yet thawed by the heater. We drove slowly on the highway, slippery in spots.

The hot coffee still seemed warm against my ribs and I squirmed cozily in my layers of wool and down. The blind would be cold and dawn would come slowly.

We turned into the rough side road. I was careful not to miss the lane toward the river, its two tracks white with fresh snow. When we had stopped by the creek we stood silent outside the little truck for a moment, listening to the mutter of running water and hoping to hear ducks or geese, but we caught only the barking of a farm dog somewhere. That reminded Jack of something.

"We should have a retriever," he said. "You don't go after downed birds as fast as you used to."

I thought of the time I'd peeled to my underwear, walked through a little snow and swum after a pair of fat mallards lodged with their orange feet up against a clump of grass. It had been years ago and I had no intention of repeating that performance.

"You'd be better off if you'd think more about Labs and less about pointing dogs," Jack accused. "There are lots of shots we pass up because we don't have a Lab. I'm gonna get me a Lab or a Chessie, or maybe one of those water spaniels."

He had been announcing that for years so I didn't take it too seriously. Jack's wife, Norma, had put her foot down. Two dogs were enough and if Jack wanted a Lab he'd have to give up one of his pointers.

64

"If he'd just treat them like members of the family, I wouldn't care," Norma had said. "But he treats them *better* than people. When the kids were home their milk came right after the dog food."

We got into our waders with grunts and puffing because our extra clothing made it difficult to stoop. We gathered up the ammunition, more than we could possibly use, the bags of decoys and the duck guns.

"That damned fence," Jack grumbled, his little flashlight playing along four tight strands of barbed wire.

We tossed the decoys over the fence, pushed the guns through, and crawled under like overweight bears, trying to keep the barbs out of our chest waders.

Next was the creek, friendly and shallow in daylight but dark, mysterious and ominous at night. From midstream. we heard the startled quacks and slapping wings of a little bunch of mallards that went almost straight up to clear the cottonwoods. For an instant we made out dark blobs above us.

We waded with our eyes on the white opposite bank, feeling the bottom stones with our feet; after that we came to the slough with more ducks and then to where the creek slowed and broadened toward the river. The blind was only a dark clump roofed with snow, much like the bushes along the backwater's shore, and we hurried a little with the decoys, trying to keep our hands dry as we placed the blocks in a foot of water, and sloshed back to the willow blind and its improvised seats.

Once there was a hissing rush when birds set their wings over the decoys and then hurried on to fade from hearing. We heard Canada geese going high and following the river, their honks and softer gabbling sparse and unhurried.

Dawn was gradual but there was a point when we knew shooting time had arrived although we checked our watches to be sure. The decoys showed plainly out there, bobbing a little in a chill breeze and collecting a few small flakes of snow. We never saw the two green-winged teal until they plummeted from nowhere and struck the water with loud plops to sit with stretched necks and eye the decoys with suspicious disapproval.

"Let's let them go," Jack said, and a few moments later they left almost as suddenly as they had arrived. We swung our guns at them.

"They look easy when you aren't going to shoot," Jack said.

A flock of mallards went over high, too many birds to be interested in our little slough and dozen decoys, but I quacked hopefully on the call.

"You sound better," said Jack, who has been critical of my duck calling for twenty years, "but if any look as if they might try to come in you leave that damned thing alone. It's hard enough to get birds into this puddle without you squawking at them."

Jack is getting older and I am very tolerant of him.

There was a speck low against the gray sky, coming fast, and it became a duck, then a big duck, then a mallard, then a drake, and he set his wings briefly as if about to come in but changed his mind and headed on. Jack has missed a lot of ducks but he didn't miss that one. He stood up with his old Model 12 pumpgun with the solid rib and the shiny receiver where the bluing is worn off, and he caught the drake in a smooth swing with an ounce and a half of fives. The duck splashed and then bobbed with its feet up.

"I wish I could do that every time," he said.

Other mallards went over high, the storm pushing them from frozen potholes to the north, but they gave no sign they had seen our decoys. There were some goldeneyes that whistled past behind the blind, and we saw a young whitetail buck on down the shore fidgeting about something, perhaps a thread of our scent he couldn't quite catalog. A cock pheasant cackled over near the main river near the thick brush, and a mink prospected the far side of our backwater, appearing and disappearing in shoreline growth.

They say that great industries have had their beginnings in

duck blinds and that national policy has been influenced
there, but Jack and I have never talked about such things as
far as I can remember. We once decided that number five shot
is a pretty good compromise between sixes and fours and we
concluded that manufacturers should test their new waders
better, but I don't know who Jack voted for in any presidential
election.

"There are no bad days in a duck blind," Jack said. "Everybody likes pretty weather but ducks generally fly better when
it's stormy. When I was younger I used to think I could hunt
ducks every day forever but now that I don't work any more
there's one thing missing—a day like this would be more fun if
you could take it off from something. When I don't work I
don't appreciate leisure, I guess.

"And now that I'm past seventy," Jack said, rubbing a speck
of mud from his gunstock, "I find there's a new problem in
growing older. When I was forty I couldn't do the things I did
when I was twenty but I didn't care because I didn't *want* to
do the things I did when I was twenty. But now that I'm seventy I wish I could still do the things I did when I was forty or
fifty."

Jack doesn't go sheep hunting any more and he doesn't
wade the deeper, faster trout and steelhead rivers.

At around noon we stood up and got the kinks out of our
muscles and then we waded out after the decoys. As they always do in the sporting calendars, a little bunch of ducks,
baldpates this time, swung in low and then towered when they
saw us frozen at attention and knee-deep in cold water. It was
snowing harder and they were simply absorbed into the sky in
seconds.

"There aren't any bad days in a duck blind," Jack said
again.

⟨⟨⟨⟨⟨⟨⟨⟨⟨⟨⟨⟨⟨⟨⟨⟨⟨⟨⟨⟨ Mule Deer

THERE WERE PLENTY OF MULE DEER that November and now the rut had begun, the time when big bucks, their necks heavy and their antler tips polished, come from the high rims and the far cedar pockets to assemble their harems of does and lose some of their caution. It was trophy time, the season soon to end, and most of the year's kill was already in freezers or aging in hundreds of Western garages. As during other late hunts the weather was important.

The snow began some time during the night, hard-driven particles riding a wind from Idaho and coming down from the peaks into a Montana valley that was already sheathed in the beginnings of winter.

Before dawn we chained up the truck, rolling gingerly about in our heavy clothing, and when we forded the creek we broke noisily through fresh ice and the willows were white with the new snow. The winding trail went steeply upward then and we left the valley ranch lights far below. With daylight the wind strengthened, swirling ghost forms of white ahead of us, sometimes hiding the two faint tracks, hard-frozen and lumpy.

When we came to the point where the road curved below a rounded sage knob there were drifts that slowed us and finally stopped us completely, so we worked with shovels and went through in jerks and stalls, looking backward apprehensively as our tracks began to fill behind us. We'd have to get out early that day, we said.

But the snow lessened for a time as I slipped on my rucksack and loaded my rifle to work carefully along a high ridge and watch a canyon with my glasses. I stayed a little back from the edge and I paid special attention to pockets that were shielded from the wind, but I saw no deer for more than

an hour. There were occasional tracks, mostly almost snow-filled, but finally I found fresh ones made by a dozen deer and going down into the canyon. There were the dainty prints of fawns, larger heart-shaped ones that must have been made by adult does, and a set of broad, splayed ones that meant a big buck traveling behind the others and leaving long marks where he had dragged his toes.

The trail disappeared around a bulge of the canyon's wall, still going downward, but I hesitated to follow, for it would be a steep drag if I made a kill down there. I stayed with the ridge a little farther but saw nothing more, and I came back to the trail and started down, gauging the altitude I was losing. It would be difficult to bring any deer up but it was still early and there was always the pack frame back in the truck. Two trips? Four? Perhaps there was a way to take the truck part-way down. I could decide later if I found the buck and he was really big.

I was already out of sight of my ridge top when I met the first deer of the day—a blocky four-pointer with no does of his own, and he glared at me without fear. He ripped at a juniper with his antlers, then must have caught a thread of my scent and grudgingly turned to climb away from my course. I told myself that if such a belligerent rascal had no does there must be giants in the canyon.

The canyon broadened and broke into a hilly valley with only scattered timber but heavy sage, and I crossed other deer trails going down toward a creek with a few aspen patches. It was ground I had never covered before and I checked my compass. I was only half an hour of hard climbing from the truck, I decided, and went farther down.

The deer were in a sheltered spot near the creek, having moved there from some intuition of approaching storm. There were about fifty of them, nibbling among sage and willows, and they were broken into half a dozen bands, each with its presiding buck or two. There were three trophy bucks, the largest quite near as I hunched above him in the sage no more than 150 yards away. He carried the heaviest rack I had ever seen and I prepared to shoot—but there was no hurry. His head went down as he crowded one of his does and I moved cautiously, hoping to fire from a sitting position. The big rack came up and my buck looked straight at me—a calendar deer with his legs and lower body hidden by sage. I would have to hurry, I thought—no time now to find a place to sit where I could see through the sage—and I lifted the rifle as smoothly as possible. Be sure. Not the neck. Back of the shoulder.

But the scope's eyepiece was blocked by a blob of snow and I hurriedly wiped it away. Still the wind held and the buck lost interest. In a valley full of deer and blowing snow he had decided I was only another deer—possibly a rival buck too far away to be a problem for the moment—and he turned back toward his harem.

Then the snow came much harder, making the deer only dark blobs below me, and I found a perfect spot to shoot from. Wait for a lull. Make a perfect shot. The crosshairs were bold against the dull scene.

But it would be foolish to shoot. Far back down the trail the track was blowing full. It would mean shoveling, even now. It was too late.

The big buck watched me again as I began to climb out and I looked back at him when I stopped to pant from exertion. The truck was farther away then I had thought, and as I neared it I saw no way of bringing it closer to the slope. We used the shovels again when we came to the bad spot and it was worse than before, even plowing downhill.

The storm grew and it was a long while before the high road was open again—probably not until spring.

‹‹‹‹‹‹‹‹‹‹‹‹‹‹‹‹‹‹‹‹‹Argentina

I HAVEN'T HAD A LETTER from Jorge lately but there should be one any day now, and I look forward to it, for Jorge's letters carry the feel of clean wind coming down from the Andes. His letters are both funny and nostalgic, the good-natured work of a brilliant man who toys happily with a language he learned from American movies.

Jorge took Fred Terwilliger and me fishing in Argentina after months of correspondence. He'd ordered some fishing tackle from Fred, who is in the tackle business, and somehow we now talk of "going fishing with Jorge," putting it that way instead of "fishing in Argentina" or "fishing in Patagonia."

He met us at the airport in Buenos Aires, introducing himself from the terminal's observation platform as Fred and I walked from the plane. He did it by a graphic mimicry of fly casting (without rod) and then scooped us into his quick little touring sedan, luggage, rods and all, airport personnel seeming to be in the spirit of the thing and evidently sorry they couldn't all come along. It was only luck, Jorge said, that he'd known when we were coming. There was a postal strike of some kind and an airline strike was pending.

Checked into El Presidente Hotel in a bustle of arrangements, we found ourselves late at night at a restaurant hangout of motorcar racers, eating gourmet food and very drunk from the local beverages Jorge insisted we sample on top of the more prosaic things we ordered. Jorge did not dine with us. He was leaving.

Take the early-morning plane to Neuquén, he said, and he would meet us there with the car. From there we would go fishing.

How far? Jorge mentally juggled kilometers and miles. About six hundred miles.

It was eleven o'clock and even the exotic drinks were unable to dim such logistic problems. How fast would he drive?

Again the kilometer-to-miles pause and the matter-of-fact estimate of a hundred miles an hour with occasional interruptions for gauchos or sheep on the road. I worried about Jorge and didn't sleep very much, but when we arrived at Neuquén next morning we waited only a few minutes. No problem, Jorge said, except for a broken oil pan. He'd patched it himself. No problem. As we hurtled off toward the mouth of the Chimehuin River, legendary home of giant brown trout, I contemplated my own probable reaction to a cracked oil pan in the dead of night on a lonely road.

Jorge was in the motion-picture business, photographing all sorts of auto races all over the world. He used to be a dentist but gave it up for racing cars and fly fishing. He also guided fishermen. Jorge took us over endless miles of Argentina's trout streams, but we kept coming back to the Chimehuin, where the faithful waded deep in the river's source at Lake Huechulafquen's outlet. The big fish did not always strike; in fact they might not always be at the *boca*, but when they were there some of them were huge and Jorge wanted big fish.

Leave Jorge for a short hike to another spot and he'd say, "Feesh a big one!"

"I hate leetle feesh!" he kept saying.

In the thousands of miles of country roads it seemed routine for Jorge to wave at acquaintances, seemingly tantamount to a New Jersey tourist casually saluting someone he knew on a back road of Arizona he'd not traveled for years before—or ever.

He discussed politics lightly and minimized South American revolutions.

"You do not understand, Charlee," he said. "The revolution here is not the great war. The general's telephone rings and the general answer it.

" 'Ow many soldiers you have?' another general says.

" 'I 'ave two hundred soldiers,' the general says.

" 'I have two hundred and fifty soldiers,' the other general says.

" 'Okay,' says the first general. 'You win. Who is the new *presidente?*"

There was the day when we fished the broad river sweeping very near to the barracks full of soldiers. While Fred and I waded in and I looked apprehensively at the compound so close to us, I saw what I had feared—a grim soldier approaching our car with a submachine gun. To me, most soldiers with submachine guns are grim. Jorge was tinkering with his tackle there. He did not expect big feesh in that section of river and he always tinkered with his tackle when the feesh were leetle.

I missed a rainbow's flashing rise and watched. The soldier talked briefly with Jorge and then hurried back to the compound, going faster than when he had approached. We fished uneasily and Jorge worked over his endless knots two hundred yards away.

The sun came down and gauchos rode up a distant mountain in the dust from their horses and dogs. When we had reeled in and reached the car I asked Jorge about the soldier.

Oh, the soldier had told him we must leave, Jorge said, but he had asked the soldier how the revolution was going and the soldier had heard of no revolution. Neither had Jorge, but he had explained to the soldier that the revolution was important in Buenos Aires.

"The communications are not good here," Jorge said. "The soldier went back to the headquarters to tell about the revolution and the general there is now wait for the telephone to ring. We will fish another place tomorrow; a good place I know."

Jorge is a naturalist, but the birds and animals of Argentina are hard to translate to English. A "worm that owns his own house" is, of course, a snail.

Do not admire anything or Jorge will get it for you. Our luggage increased alarmingly as days went on but the little car somehow made room for it.

We were not after large fish only. Take us to a place where there are more but smaller fish, we pleaded. It was not until our trip was ending that Jorge did that. It was higher in the mountains and the road dust was inches deep. It was cold boulder water and a two-pound brown trout struck my streamer on my first cast. A somewhat smaller rainbow took the second and Jorge watched sadly.

"I hate leetle feeshes," he said, and began tinkering with his tackle.

It was late when Fred and I climbed from that river to the road and started back to the car in the elation that goes with perfect fishing. The dusty road was light in the rising moon, and two flat-hatted gauchos, riding high on their gaucho saddles, met us suddenly on a curve of the road, their big dogs dropping away to the far side of the horses, uneasy near the specters we must have been with chest waders, fishing vests and gleaming rods. I saw the wide eyes of the men as they faced us and I mumbled some sort of greeting, heard a shy response and then cowered as the horses and dogs broke up in barking, plunging disorder. May they never again have to meet fly fishermen in the moonlight.

Jorge loves to drive and he does it with the quick, decisive moves of the road racer.

"I am not fast but I am accurate," he said. Perhaps he meant "precise," but the word he used is somehow better. When he wanted something different for dinner at one of the inns we visited he expertly struck down a big hare with the car, a move comparable to gathering a tomato from the garden. At other times he smoothly avoided hares in the road.

He drove with his arms fairly straight, and his touring skills had been sharpened by Buenos Aires traffic, a national participation sport. When I spelled him at the wheel on an open road he explained that I would be killed the first day in

Buenos Aires. I had no daring, he explained, and defensive driving in Argentina, he went on, requires a good offense.

But I emphasize the driving part because on the day we were to return from Buenos Aires, Jorge overslept and was very late in picking us up at the hotel. I had jittered about the lobby as our flight departure time came nearer. It was a long way to the airport and an airline strike was about to begin. Already we were days later than we had originally intended to return. Although we did not know it, none of our letters had reached the United States.

Finally, a desk clerk told me: "Now it would be impossible for anyone to reach the airport on time. You must stay now."

It was almost ten minutes later that Jorge arrived in another fleet little touring car (he was part owner of an automobile agency), a little less confident, I thought, than usual.

It was a long way to the airport, through Buenos Aires, and we waited for nothing.

"If you stop for the police, you are in a mess," Jorge philosophized. We did not stop for the police and there were times when we screamed along the wrong side of the boulevard medians.

"You must watch far ahead," Jorge said.

I remember best the moment when the dodging cars and gaping pedestrians dropped suddenly behind and the road ahead was open. Already we were going eighty miles an hour and the little car thrust forward.

"We have made it, Fred," Jorge said, and shook hands with Fred. I do not know if Fred's hand was as damp as mine.

The jet was ready for takeoff but the airline people scurried about under a shower of Jorge's Spanish. A man weighed our luggage and remonstrated but stepped back from Jorge's staccato reply and then penciled resignedly on his clipboard.

"Nine kilos is nothing!" Jorge proclaimed in English, and Fred and I stumbled across the field with our wine bottles, our rods and bags, our packages of maté tea and our Indian rugs.

Nearing the big airplane's nose we learned Jorge had penetrated airport security and was still with us. A hatch opened in the pilot's compartment.

"Jorge! Jorge!" shouted the captain, and we scuttled up the stairs for old-home week with the crew while amazed travelers postponed their flight to Miami. We were high over snowy ranges before I settled back and laughed at Fred.

I hope Jorge's most recent letter hasn't been lost.

‹‹‹‹‹‹‹‹‹‹‹‹‹‹‹‹‹‹‹‹‹‹‹‹ It's a Living

A WHILE BACK MY WIFE was calculating her way through a supermarket and the owner of the place came up, introduced himself and asked:

"Is it worthwhile to write that outdoor stuff? If I can get paid enough to make it worthwhile I might turn out some myself. I hunt a lot."

Now this is getting pretty personal when you're talking to a gal who has been living off outdoor writing for twenty-five years, but Debie smiled and said sometimes it was worthwhile and sometimes it wasn't. I guess the man was satisfied. He'd probably have been offended if Debie had asked him whether he really thought there was any sense to piling up all those groceries and expecting people to buy them.

We fish and hunt a lot. We also travel quite a bit and we do a heck of a lot of work. It's true that we get some special considerations when we go fishing or hunting. Many people help us out from the goodness of their hearts, realizing we must get some information, catch some fish and get some game. The other side of this dime is that many of them are very eager for me to foul up, which I often do. Some of them secretly hope I will miss all the birds or be unable to cast a fly past my boot toes. The heat is on, especially if I'm in a strange land with total strangers, and I've seen many a knowing smile as I dug out my rod or gun. This means that although I don't have to be a champion I have to know how to load my gun or string up my rod without getting my fingers caught. It will be more fun for many of them if they can learn I'm a complete phony. The host is likely to be the local hotshot with the checkering worn smooth on his shotgun or with a deep groove where his thumb clamps his fly rod. I don't expect to beat him, because beating a man at his own local game is nearly impossible and poor

79

public relations anyway—but I want to hit a bird or catch a fish.

I have pretty well given up studying things not related to my business, which means that when you take me indoors I'm kind of stupid. I was thrown in with some other writers not long ago and one of them, a novelist, asked me what I thought about a certain book. I had never heard of it. The guy who asked me has made a fortune writing novels and for the movies but I haven't read but one of his books. I gave up general reading when I went into the outdoor business and forced myself to take a reading interest only in outdoor subjects. Some of the sharper characters seem to know everything without studying. Not me.

I enjoy hunting or fishing two hundred days a year and I also enjoy taking pictures of others doing it. It is not the constant lark you might expect. Let's take yesterday:

I got up a little late; no clock to punch. I went fishing to try to catch warmouth perch on popping bugs in a place where they are hard to catch on popping bugs. The idea was to catch them or find out why I couldn't. I didn't catch them and I don't know why so I came home at five p.m. with no warmouth perch and no story. Dry run except for a nice picture I made of some crappie fishermen.

I cleaned up the boat, put away my tackle, ate dinner and worked over the typewriter for two hours. By that time it was nine o'clock and I knocked off "work." But I didn't sit in front of the TV or go to a night club or visit neighbors. I sat down to study a book on the eutrophication of deepwater impoundments. I was not particularly interested in the eutrophication of deepwater impoundments but figured I should know more about it if I was going to write about fishing in them. By midnight I was pretty interested in it. I have forced myself into getting interested in anything related to my field. I started doing that in 1934 and it comes easier than it used to—the interest, not the learning.

At midnight I went to bed because I was going fishing this morning.

This is a pleasant way to make a living—for me. Lots of people would like to fish for warmouth perch or shoot a few quail, but they might not be too enthusiastic about threshing the typewriter or reading about the eutrophication of deep-water impoundments.

When I get through with this tonight I am going to read about the manufacture of German shotguns. Sounds a little dull but I think it may be nice after I get into it.

Writer's Mail >>>>>>>>>>>>>>>>>>>>>

O CCASIONAL MAIL FROM READERS makes outdoor writers feel recognized and sometimes even wanted. But there are a few letters now and then that make them feel a bit insecure in the thought that those folks out there really are a little strange. Like these:

SPECIAL SERVICE

Dear Mr. Waterman:

I have read with great interest your article on fishing with popping bugs for bass and snook. It is by far the most comprehensive article on the subject I have ever read and I am anxious to try it myself. How do you do it? Stamped envelope is enclosed.

Sincerely yours,

CAT LOVER?

Mr. Waterman:

I hope there is a special place in hell for you. Your hint that cats are natural bird killers is disgusting. Only a poor, starving waif of a kitty, abandoned by heartless people, would be forced to attack a songbird and you are trying to get our lovely pets murdered by heartless hunters.

In saying that some dogs will attack cats without training you show that you know nothing about dogs and cats. If cruel men like you would leave them alone, all dogs and cats would lie down at the fireside together but you teach dogs to kill cats.

Signed,

[In response to column stating that stray cats sometimes kill birds and that some dogs kill cats.]

EGO TRIP

Dear Mr. Waterman:

I have read an article by you in which you say that your wife caught a 3¾-pound trout on a 6-X tippet in Montana. All true angling sportsmen should be ashamed of you for writing such hogwash. I have never even done that myself.

Sincerely,

REAL ESTATE

Dear Mr. Waterman:

I have never fished but I am retiring next year and am thinking of moving to Florida. I want to buy a waterfront home where there is good fishing the year around. Please send me a list of such places.

Yours truly,

SCIENTIFIC THINKER

Dear Sir:

Do you have any plans for a lure that explodes and kills a fish when it bites? If so, how does it keep from blowing the fish's head off and losing it?

Sincerely,

SHOPPER

Dear Fishing Editor:

My husband fishes from the bank at night with a big float and I want to get him something for Christmas. Where can I get a light that he can shine on the float but will not shine between the float and him and scare the fish? I don't want the fish to see it.

Yours truly,

EXECUTIVE MEMO

Dear Mr. Waterman:

Please explain the solunar tables and tell how effective they are. Also let me know when you publish this as I am going to be away fishing in Wyoming and might not see it.

Regards,

HIDDEN GENIUS

Dear Sir:

I have had a lot of hunting and fishing experience and have had many unusual things happen to me so I am thinking of becoming a writer. Can you make a living at it?

Sincerely yours,

CONSERVATIONIST

Dear Sir:

I have seen some men catching fish and putting them back. Who should I report this to?

Yours truly,

PERPLEXED

Fishing Editor:

I want to get my husband a fishing thing for Christmas. He had three and he lost one. What is it?

Sincerely,

SCHOLAR

Dear Sir:

I have been reading your monthly articles about fishing and some of them are pretty good. I don't know all that much about fishing. Please send me information on how to fish with flies, plugs, spoons, jigs, plastic worms and live bait. What kinds of fish do you catch with these? Please explain how to use them in both fresh and salt water. What time of year is best for each kind of bait and what time of day should you use them?

Please send me a list of the best flies, plugs, spoons and plastic worms and tell me where I can buy each one as I don't know all that much about fishing. Also list the best time of the moon for each bait.

Yours,

Maine ⤞⤞⤞⤞⤞⤞⤞⤞⤞⤞⤞⤞⤞⤞⤞⤞⤞⤞⤞⤞⤞⤞⤞

Wʜᴇɴ ɪ ᴡᴀꜱ ᴀ ᴋɪᴅ ᴀɴᴅ ꜰɪʀꜱᴛ ʙᴇᴄᴀᴍᴇ addicted to outdoor magazines around 1920 it seemed that a true outdoorsman held forth in only two places—a steam-heated office in New York City and a leaky tent in Maine.

It is true that I read occasionally of forays into other parts of the country, but the real hunting and fishing were in Maine and you did it in canoes and you wore felt hats pinched to a peak at the crown with trout flies stuck in the band, even if you fished exclusively with worms. Such hats are still popular in Maine and I think part of them are the same ones.

Now, I was raised in the Midwest with little hope of ever actually getting to Maine, but I figured a careful study of Maine hunting and fishing might enhance my homely pleasures with the bobwhites of southeastern Kansas and the smallmouth bass of Missouri and Arkansas. When I collected a bobwhite I would mentally compare the thrill with what I might have felt in bagging a ruffed grouse near Millinocket, and when I landed a smallmouth from a pine johnboat near Branson, Missouri, I wondered how that compared to catching one from a canoe on the Belgrade Lakes south of Skowhegan. Later on when I began really promiscuous hunting and fishing it seemed the Maine thing never could be arranged and I figured there were too many better outdoor writers going there anyway.

I was especially interested in the smallmouth bass fishing and once wrote a letter about it to an acquaintance who lived in Portland. He answered me rather coldly and it was the last I ever heard from him. It was years later I realized it was the bass reference which had offended him. Until then I hadn't known the attitude of Maine trout fishermen toward bass. I once read an excellent book on trout, written in pleasing dignity by a Maine resident. The last page of each chapter, however, was devoted to bitter remarks about black bass and in these passages the author would completely lose his cool and write like an anarchist, implying that all black bass should be rotenoned at dead of night. I finally found out that the people who enjoy smallmouth bass in Maine don't live there.

It took me fifty years to reach Maine on the day before a June 1 bass opening. The bright lake lay deep in the granite hills and forest as I had known it would, the road winding down to it and giving intermittent views of sunny water and the gleams of white summer cottages. There were too many summer cottages, I thought. Perhaps there would be no leaky tents, or even felt hats with flies in them.

Most of the summer cottages were empty. There were wooden boats stacked on the shore and in sheds as they had been all winter, and the camp was closed. Bass opening tomorrow?

"Our summer season hasn't started yet. Bass? Oh, sure. Bass. Some people eat 'em. We could open you a cottage, I guess. Haven't really cleaned them up yet. Boats aren't in the water now. We'll get you one."

The boat was wooden, one of those ageless Maine resort boats, built for the years, and my little outboard went on where hundreds of little outboards had been clamped, the transom gouged, painted over and gouged again, but there to stay. The boat leaked, for it had dried through a Maine winter. It might tighten up slightly overnight.

It was quiet in the cottage and the moon shone on the flat lake. A single small outboard whined busily in some unseen cove. Morning was almost cloudless. There were no fishermen to be seen and I motored slowly away from the little dock, reset each spring after the weeks of ice.

The gravel bottom, shallow near the dock, deepened very gradually and the boat seemed to hang over the gravel, the clear, cool water hardly in evidence under it. Boulders showed as the water deepened, and I drifted without the engine as I approached a steep bank.

The fly rod was light for bass, for the smallmouth flies were small, and I hesitated only briefly over the aluminum fly box. There was a hair bug, impossible for me to resist although I thought a streamer would be better. The bright little powderpuff, banded in red and white, had been tied and trimmed by Tap Tapply in the perfection of careful things built for the fun of building them. I would use a bug made by a man who knew of old felt hats, ruffed grouse and New England. A little line dressing on the underside to keep it floating high.

But no smallmouth were to come darting from the steep, rocky bank—only a small largemouth which came out slowly, eyed the quivering deer-hair bristles and took with a tentative plop.

I rowed out a little to deeper water and saw the immense submerged granite chunks, showing gray-brown where the water darkened. Rather deep for the little hair bug. Now there were ripple patches on the flat calm, the early-morning spell of hazy quiet about to leave. A boat motor started somewhere.

I cast the bug to one of the great boulders, where it dropped like a giant insect, the tiny waves spreading for a few seconds before I twitched it gently.

The bass came from a dark canyon between boulders, a shadow of indefinite size, coming fast, and it took the bug still going up, showing a gleaming bronze side and spurting away— now concealed by its own surface turmoil. It was a broad bass with a fiery red eye and I best remember the shadow coming swiftly up to the little bug. There are more summer cottages now and there are more camping trailers than leaky tents, but Maine did not fail me. I went back the next year.

‹‹‹‹‹‹‹‹‹‹‹‹‹‹‹ Hunting Horses

Horses can be treacherous, even as can humans, and I am a little afraid of them. But there is something special about the mountain-hunting horse, holding his steady pace on the brittle edge of blue chasms and carrying his load of awkward hunter and strange trappings. Sometimes he plays a double role and carries panniers or man interchangeably. He lives off the wild land, and the wrangler slumbers in his sleeping bag while the horse bell tinkles and sits up cold and worried when the sound fades.

The mountain-hunting horse is only transportation until the trail is lost, the slide rock moves, or bear scent is heavy on the air. And then he is apart from mere valley and flatland prancers. He is one with a mountain wind bringing the feel of snow and the unforgotten creak and jangle of the pack string.

John Madson wrote it the way I would have liked to in a short poem:

> *His sire was Spain:*
> *His dam, the Nez-Perce.*
> *Legs forged on granite anvils;*
> *Heart forged by mountains.*
>
> *Kin to the bighorn*
> *With clever hoof and infinite eye.*
> *Drinker of the wind, the dawn-singer,*
> *Kin to the elk.*
>
> *Enduring, gaunt, rock-worn,*
> *Lacking titled rank or registry,*
> *His labors win the noble heights*
> *And the consort of eagles.*

89

For a mountain hunter to admit being a little afraid of
horses is to imply a sheltered background, a certain lack of un-
derstanding, and even weakness of character. I was almost
forty years old before I openly confessed that my craven attitude toward horses was other than healthy respect. I am much
more comfortable now that I have come clean about it. I am a
little afraid of horses.

Saying you were raised with horses is supposed to cover the
whole thing and indicate you are half cowboy and half jockey.
Hell, I was raised with horses and was kicked in the stomach
when I was five. I suppose that should have started me off as a
horse lover, but when I was ten I encountered a she-devil
named Bonnie, of all things.

I needed a saddle horse to ride five miles to school and my
father took me to a horse dealer. Dad was a good judge of
horses, having broken and worked them all of his life, but he
slipped momentarily on juvenile psychology. I picked Bonnie
from a corral full of better choices and was adamant in my se-
lection, even when she went over backward as the dealer applied a saddle. I soon learned that was only one of her colorful
habits.

Now Bonnie could buck. I fully understand that term. I
have photographed a few rodeos and I have watched Bonnie
both from aboard and from a distance. She could *buck!* I don't
know who won my four-year war with her but I recall the
words of the guy with the big hat who came to pick her up for
the horse buyer who finally got her from my father.

At the time he was dusting off his Levis in a corner of our
corral and looking for the aforementioned hat.

"That," he said admiringly, "is one sunfishin' little bitch!"

Not that Bonnie was a full-time outlaw. She could present a
sweet disposition and had "all the gaits" in addition to gleeful
sunfishing. Her bucking was a surprise that might come at any
time and without warning. The only reason I survived our
relationship was that most of her bucking was short-lived,
Bonnie feeling that if you couldn't dispose of a passenger

quickly there was no use wasting effort. If you were still there after a brief explosion she would snort in resignation and get back to the saddle-horse business. Of course, if you brought her in from a long period on pasture she could really put her mind to bucking, as she did when Dad finally sold her.

Having read most of Zane Grey's work and attended numerous William S. Hart movies I was not about to admit fear of Bonnie, even after she pinned me in a stall and tried to bite my arm off. I was even proud of the scarred saddle resulting from her occasional backflips. My father must have understood my ordeal and perhaps he thought it was building my character.

I have since reasoned that a muscular creature weighing a thousand pounds and generations removed from any animal dangerous to it should not come apart at sight of a two-pound rabbit. I am sure horses sense my distrust, and just in case they can actually smell fear as some authorities say, I try to mount from downwind.

There was the time I got up on a borrowed horse at a field trial, wearing two cameras around my neck. Horses in my experience are evidently annoyed by clacking shutters and film-winding sounds, and this one kept up a dance that distracted the judges and made my pictures fuzzy. So some solicitous official brought up an ancient plug of sleepy disposition and suggested I accept a steadier platform, guaranteed gentle but possibly unable to keep up with the field for very long. I was grateful until the gray-muzzled ancient took a slanting look at my cameras, snorted froth and stood on his hind legs.

There have been exceptions, of course. There was Otto, who lived in Canada, spent his winters in the wild and had a short, ragged mane from grazing under conifer branches when the snow was too deep elsewhere. Otto was a bit short in the leg, and mountain horsemen distrust the stocky build as being hard riding over the long haul, but when I drew Otto for a tough hunt in upended country it took only a few minutes to learn I was aboard a mountain treasure. To Otto, choice of the

best footing seemed automatic. There was the patch of bottomless muskeg where a packhorse went down and the wrangler came up with appropriate phraseology to unload him. And a moment later my fellow hunter found himself afoot with his new Vibram-soled hunting boots hidden in ooze while his horse wallowed like a stranded manatee, the hunter gingerly reaching for his custom rifle as its boot began to disappear under his unhappy mount. The outfitter, tugging at his rope, charged up to change our course, but Otto and I were already on the bad spot and I clawed for my rifle and saddlebags.

"Aw, leave Otto alone," snapped the wrangler, so I sat like a wax horseman and Otto walked carefully across the entire sinkhole with pitying glances at his mired associates. Once across and on solid ground, Otto sighed in boredom and nibbled a bush.

"Otto never mires," grunted the wrangler, standing over one of his charges and looking for a club.

"Get up, you flat-footed son of a bitch!"

Otto and I waited until the pack string was rerouted around the soft spot and had joined us. Later that day a ruffed grouse boomed up under Otto's feet and I clutched the saddle horn but Otto just looked casually at the spot the bird had flushed from as if to say they sometimes take off in pairs in that country.

Then we met the rutting bull moose in a brushy clearing. The bull, not being long on eyesight, hadn't caught our scent and evidently thought he had met a whole herd of lady moose escorted by an unfriendly bull. I did my version of a quick draw with a nine-pound rifle, although I didn't want the rag-horned grunter. Otto stopped and casually reached for a bush. He seemed to be waiting for something.

"Look out, here comes Badger!" somebody yelled and a big gray packhorse crashed past us, panniers and all, ears back and teeth bared in wheezing fury.

"Badger doesn't like moose," a guide said. "Otto lets him do the fighting."

I noticed everybody accepted Otto as an equal. A guide dropped back from his point position one day.

"Your blanket feel okay, Otto?" he inquired. I thought Otto nodded, but it must have been my imagination.

A rifle tends to pull the saddle to one side a little and a horseman once told me you could learn to ride just a bit off center to counterbalance it. With Otto I did this with great care. I'd never forgive myself if he got a sore back.

For a while I thought I had suddenly become quite a horseman, but each hunter on that trip rode three different horses, letting two rest each day, and when I used my second mount I learned nothing had changed. The other horses and I maintained the usual uneasy relationship.

Wherever old Otto is now I hope the grass is green and the winters mild.

The late Ed Welch of Montana was a horseman of unusual stamp. He had a special way with horses. Oh, Ed could stay up there if one came unwound, but he didn't consider himself a bronc buster. He was a horse trainer, and although he built his own rifles and believed in a minute of angle for his favorites, he really went hunting to use his horses. I learned that the first time he took a few days off from his Bozeman sporting goods store and led me into the mountains. We met a good muley buck face to face on the trail at dusk. The horses pricked their ears and waltzed nervously.

"Wonder what's wrong with these fool horses?" Ed said, studying the deer with appreciation. "I don't see anything."

Ed was a practical joker. They were harmless pranks and the amount of trouble he went to just didn't matter. The preparation was as much fun as the result. He'd been an automobile mechanic at one time and he asked my help in a little project. He wanted to dismantle an automobile and horsepack it piece by piece to the top of Sage Mountain in the Gallatin Forest, then reassemble it at the uppermost point, many miles from any road. He'd leave out the engine and other heavy parts, he said, and would get a clean-looking car from a wrecking firm.

"Sage Mountain is so high the eagles rest and puff awhile before going over it," Ed said. "Can't you imagine some poor guy crawling up there tired out and about at the end of his rope and then coming on a shiny Chevrolet where there isn't even a foot trail?"

"The forest service might get us for littering up the mountain," I suggested.

"Whaddya mean, littering?" Ed said. "This would be a real nice-looking car. Do you think we should keep a current license on it?"

Ed's health failed shortly after that. Maybe we wouldn't have done it anyway, but sometimes I can imagine that car parked at the high end of the knife ridge on top. We could have done it in a week, Ed said.

He loved to play the part of a nice guy just a little off his rocker on certain subjects. There was the time we happened to meet two other hunters at a fork in the trail and rode with them for a couple of miles. The conversation turned to rifles.

"I use a .270 Weatherby myself," Ed said. "But they tell me a .35 Remington is better in the brush, and since it's kind of thick up in here I use .35 Remington ammunition in my Weatherby."

There was a brief silence after which the two other hunters pulled off the trail, mumbling something about deciding to work their way across a canyon.

When we stopped in an elk camp for coffee (Ed was a social hunter), Ed said he'd always wondered about that business of leading a horse to water but not being able to make him drink.

"It got to preying on my mind," Ed told the camp cook and a wrangler. "So we roped that stud and threw him down in Sage Creek. We hogtied him and sat on his head. He drank all right, but it was a lot of trouble."

The wrangler finished his coffee and walked away eyeing Ed's stallion. The cook was still sitting there by the fire look-

ing into his cup when we left. Even the batwing chaps Ed
made me wear didn't make me feel like a roper, but I am naturally bowlegged and who knows?

It was dawn and Ed sat on a jutting rimrock with two of his
friends and glassed a gaping canyon almost filled with curling
mist.

"There," hissed Ed, "is the biggest bull elk I ever saw. Bust
'em, Bill. I've already got a good head. Wup! The fog has him
covered."

Bill nervously pushed his rifle muzzle forward and stared at
gray blankness.

"That's a good five hundred yards," Ed said breathlessly.
"Don't try it with that thing. I'll go back to the horses and get
a real rifle."

"Don't take too long," fussed Bill. "That fog'll lift any
minute."

Ed was gone for several minutes but the fog held until he
got back.

"Make the first one count," urged Ed. "You'll have to hold
over, even with this."

And he pressed a child's airgun into his buddy's sweating
palms. It was the only weapon Ed took on that trip but there
was no bull elk anyway.

Ed did have some remarkably tough horses, and his idea of a
perfect hunt was to camp comfortably at the edge of game
country and ride in and out each day, going up and in as far as
fifteen miles. You didn't get much hunting that way but you
sure got a lot of riding, which was his real joy.

On one trip to his beloved Gallatin Sage Creek country we
actually lived in a motel down on the highway. Each morning
we'd load two of Ed's super horses in a trailer, pull them in as
far as we could with four-wheel-drive and ride on from there.
We'd pass camps that had been set up for days and when we'd

stop for a social hour somebody would ask where we were camped, obviously noting our clean shirts and fresh shaves.

"Oh, we're camped at Rainbow Ranch down on the highway," Ed would explain. "No snakes or anything there."

Of course a hunter who had ridden in with a pack string would have a hard time believing that, since he'd spent the better part of a day on the trail just getting to camp.

Ed's horses moved fast and it was on one of those daily ride-in hunts that I met Lady. Lady was a tall gray, easy-gaited and good at choosing her footing. I rode her while Ed seemed to enjoy a squealy, combative little Appaloosa stallion, not exactly first choice for rough country, but Ed was "training" him.

Ed's system for training a mountain horse was to tease it constantly until it no longer feared any strange sound or motion. Ed continually flicked the Appaloosa's ears with a stick. He slapped the saddle fork. He reached back and cuffed the stud's abbreviated rump. He tugged its mane and switched its legs very lightly. At first the snorty little villain danced, tried to run and took threatening stances, but finally he began to accept the slaps, gouges and strange noises, being almost tractable except when we neared other horses, at which time he squealed challenges to any and all and reverted to dancing and blowing with his ears back. Ed thought this was very entertaining but rode wide around pack trains, aware of the equine riots that might occur.

Something happened between me and Lady. Lady decided to buckjump a little—not too bad, just a tooth-jarring series of stiff-legged hops, but since her form was almost perfect I suspected she knew some things she wasn't showing. She did this little number several times so I figured she was just feeling things out, and my being naturally suspicious of equine foibles, some of the fun began to go out of my trip. A rodeo on a mountain trail is serious business for me. Ed looked a little worried.

Then we found a big hunting party just coming out at the highway as we prepared to trailer the horses one evening. Lady was tied to a tree and when I walked over to get her there were two men standing looking at her. They were lean, stringy men in big hats with big belt buckles and packer boots and they had the dust and sweat of a long hunt about them. I heard them as I came up.

"Don't tell me I don't know that hussy," one said. "Look at that brand!"

And it all flashed before me—the stories of the miracle worker Ed Welch and how he bought outlaw horses and made Christians of them with knowhow and patience. And maybe some of them backslid a little. Would he fool me after all this time?

"Mister, you ridin' that mare?" one of the men asked.

"Yeah, that's mine," I said.

"Quite a hoss, ain't she?"

"Well, yes, I guess so," I sparred. "She sure is tough."

"Yep, sure is. And man, when the Curly Q sold her she was one man-bustin' hell splitter."

And I turned under their probing eyes and walked back to Ed with my bow legs and my batwing chaps.

"After this," I said with my voice carefully controlled, "I'll ride the Appaloosa."

"Good." Ed grinned. "I guess Lady's been out on grass too long."

The Appaloosa squealed and grunted and it seemed funny to be on a spotted little horse with a ski-slide rump, but he never bucked. I kept looking over at Ed, grinning, a little watchful, flipping the rein ends and talking to Lady. He was training her all over again.

A horse story can go from fun to dead serious in moments.

Coming down the mountain we spoke little and tried to keep our voices soft as we looked for game on the higher slopes, in the grassy parks among the pines and in the aspen patches, their yellow leaves almost gone now and their trunks making vertical white streaks. Four mounted men were too many for a quiet passage, and we moved with the squeaks and thumps of horses going steeply downward.

We watched the horses' ears for sign of game scent on the chilling evening breeze that turned dead leaves in the trail and moved sage on lumps of the mountain's shoulder. We shivered a little when the sun was suddenly behind a distant ridge, feeling the cold dampness of sweat that had gathered earlier as we hunted on foot, and mountain nightfall was near, even though the snowy peaks still sparkled. As we passed through timber patches the pines murmured the sound that can be lonely or comforting depending on human spirit, and far below was the tinkle of a tiny creek heard only occasionally.

The trail became fainter and wider as fading trails do, and when we reached the first talus the track was no longer there. And now the pitch steepened sharply and we slid out of our saddles, bone-tired and already stiffened from the ride that had followed a hard day, and began to lead the horses down toward camp, unseen and far below. A tired horse slipped and grunted and the way was even steeper.

"This is the wrong way down," Ike said from down ahead, and we stopped for a few moments but went on slowly.

The shale rock changed to loose, hat-sized boulders and we angled off to ease our descent.

"We couldn't get back up now," Ike said.

Now he was the leader, like it or not, and he stumbled to keep ahead or above his horse but made it continue downward. Then the horse second in line fell, its shoes striking sparks as it went to its knees. The man leading it stood still for a moment, bracing himself with a hand on a boulder.

"Get him up," Ike said.

But the big gelding clawed himself to his feet without urging. Ike's mare went down next and for a moment she panicked and lunged.

"Whoa," said Ike as he pulled his rifle from the saddle scabbard. "All right, now, let's go."

Then the mare firmly muscled herself up and we went on.

A horse named Cody went down behind me and I saw a long scar appear on the figured rifle stock protruding from the boot.

"I spent a lotta dough on that piece of wood," grumbled its owner, reaching for his treasure and sliding the sling on his shoulder. "Get up, Cody. There's no oats up here."

There were other falls but my Rube kept his feet.

"You don't ride much," someone had said. "You can have Rube. He's good in the hills."

Rube was catty on the tumbled boulders—not just quick or graceful but crouched like a great bay hunting cat, his ears forward, his eyes rolling, not in fear but to find his next foothold, almost patting his feet as he felt for solid spots.

We were on the canyon floor less than an hour later and the horses had bloody hocks, but there was nothing seriously wrong. The sun was gone from the high peaks and Ike lighted a match to check his gear. The binocular strap I'd hardly noticed earlier was cutting into my neck. One hand was scraped and I'd bruised both shins.

I remember Ike standing in the dark with his feet wide apart looking up at the mountain outlined in stars and a sliver of moon.

"We came down the wrong way," he said. "The trail is over there somewhere."

«««««««««««««««««««««««Bluegills

THERE ARE FAMOUS BASS FISHERMEN, famous tarpon fishermen, and famous trout fishermen. As far as I know, there are no famous bluegill fishermen. If you want fame, trophies, or riches, the bluegill is not the way to go.

I keep reading about sportsmen who come into a clubhouse and savor the memories of a wonderful day on the water or afield, along with strong drink. They toast the memories of big bass, bobwhite quail, Canada geese, or sailfish. Apparently bluegill fishermen do not drink much, or they do not have clubhouses. Anyway, it is not very stylish to go misty-eyed over an escaping bluegill, and if taxidermists counted on bluegill business, they'd starve.

I have given considerable thought to the reasons why bluegill fishermen are not held in high repute, and I think one of the main factors is clothing. What does a bluegill fisherman dress like? See? You have no mental picture of a bluegill fisherman.

A trout fisherman worth his salt wears waders and a fishing vest. Up until lately the bass fishermen were a little nondescript, but now that the jumpsuit has come into its own, along with all those colorful patches advertising bass clubs, outboard motors, plastic worms, and rods, the bass fisherman is a real individual. A deepwater ocean angler has all sorts of sporty togs.

I once thought I would add a little class to bluegill fishing, so I went and caught some bluegills while wearing a fly fisherman's vest and a canvas hat with a wood-duck feather in the band, but it didn't catch on.

There is a thing the grouse hunters have up in New England—a lot of them wear neckties while hunting, I am told. It

might be that a necktie would help the bluegill fisherman's image, but I have not tried it.

It is a lot of fun to catch bluegills on a very light bamboo fly rod, and I have done quite a bit of that, although some people say it is a waste of a hundred-dollar stick to catch bluegills on it. Since I am pretty well south of where it could get me into trouble, I might say that an eight-ounce bluegill feels much the same as an eight-ounce trout on a hundred-dollar rod.

I'll take my bluegill fishing deep in the South along in May, and the river should be slow and dark. Small clumps of water hyacinths should drift on the main current in eerie quiet and big banks of them should clog the backwaters and coves where the lily pads are—but down South you call the pads "bonnets." I like the oaks to be high and carrying Spanish moss that swings smoothly in the evening breeze and sometimes one of the bigger pendants jerks convulsively where a gray squirrel has gotten in a hurry about his squirrel business.

There should be cypress knees here and there along the shore and there would be a couple of places where big trees have fallen landward and their root systems have pulled loose from the bottom and left deep pockets against the edge. There should be a few clumps of dead limbs along the bank, each having collected a wad of hyacinths, and there should be turtles and possibly a moccasin on a half-sunken log, its upper surface partly covered with resurrection fern, bright-green from the afternoon thundershower.

I'll choose a fairly small boat, maybe a johnboat that moves easily under the oars, and we'll use a little outboard motor to get to the place we know the bluegills are. Then we'll tip the motor up and we'll put a couple of drops of oil on the rowlocks to keep them quiet, and by this time the river will begin to feel like bluegills. There'll be pink tips on the thunderheads and a row of white ibis (down there you call them curlews) will come up the river heading to roost, and when they see us just as they round the bend they'll flare up and break formation a little, then get back in line after they've passed us.

By now the breeze will pretty well have died out and a pileated woodpecker will sound as if he's using a mallet back in the river swamp. The limpkin will be hard to see standing there in the shadows with a big snail in his beak, but a great blue heron will fly off with a sepulchral squawk that seems to be a complaint and a promise of doomsday at the same time. We'll hope to see a pair of wood ducks and possibly hear them squeal as they fly through open spaces in what looks like solid timber, and at about bluegill time we'll hear a pair of barred owls sounding like a dozen birds in the timber. By then the fish crows will be going home but looking for some last bit of evening deviltry.

The little bug will have white rubber legs, and if I row you can peel off some freshly dressed fly line and feel it just a little greasy in your fingers. Your reel click will sound loud and I'll try to slide you along the shore as quietly as possible so that you can drop the little bug against the edge of the hyacinths, close to the tree roots, right on top of the bonnets, and back under some swooping branches that almost hide a rotting stump.

If the panfish are going to stir we'll probably hear them first in tiny plops back under the hyacinth rafts and very small fish will make sucking sounds in the floating hyacinth roots where they can find all sorts of things. There will be little circles of wake where something is busy under a clump of bonnets and we might change to a bigger bug if we hear a bass strike, but we won't be fooled by the double plop of a rolling gar or the splash downstream where an anhinga has decided to dive off his perch instead of flying away as a bird is supposed to.

Don't hurry the little rubber-legged bug. When it strikes the water with the slightest plop you can leave it while the rubber legs wave a little before you twitch it. Watch for a bulge in the water as a bluegill (they call them bream down there) comes out to examine it. If it's a small bulge he might tug at the rubber legs, but if it's a big plate-sized fish, blue-black from living in that stained water, he might take it with a bang that reminds you of a bass and you can lift the tip promptly and feel him dart toward the shore and then swing out under pressure to go around and around under the dipping rod tip as you haul in line to scoop him up.

Your heart won't be in your throat and your wrist probably won't ache, but we'll take our bluegill fishing down in Florida along in May and the little rod will feel much as it does when it bows to brown trout or grayling.

‹‹‹‹‹‹‹‹‹‹‹‹‹‹‹‹‹‹‹‹‹‹‹‹‹‹‹‹‹‹ Toby

Taber, alberta—in southern Alberta the giant stubble fields are bordered by low sand hills that reach a horizon broken rarely by a windmill or an abandoned homestead.

The coyotes that drive the bird dogs wild at night slide like gray shadows along the arroyos ahead of the hunting rigs, and the mallards jump noisily from ditches and potholes or hiss into cornfields in clouds just before sunset. Geese and swans add their high-altitude conversations at morning and evening as they go out from the lakes to feed.

But this year the sharptail grouse and pheasants are scarce, hunting is hard, and Hungarian partridges are very wild as they tend to be when the prairie winds drive hard. Such conditions are hard on Toby, the German shorthair, and Pat, the inquisitive Brittany. Van, the big setter, is disgusted and tired of the whole thing.

Toby is only eight months old and he is a little uncertain of what to point and where to look but he tries hard and Bud encourages him.

"Good dog, Toby."

Pat, the Brittany, has never been noted for deep thought and he has succumbed to the investigation of magpies and all sorts of mysterious holes in the sandy ground. He is more than a year old and handsome, but no great credit to his breed where bird finding is concerned. He is thinking of jackrabbits.

But a sharptail goes up wide, barely in range, and Bud swings the hammer double he insists on using and kills it high in the air where Toby sees it fall.

"Fetch, Toby."

And Toby goes, a dark streak of enthusiasm across the dry, tan grass and scoops up the bird. This he knows about.

But fifty yards behind him the vagrant Pat has snuffled up a

big jackrabbit and gives joyful chase in frantic, yippy barks. The rabbit, loafing in second gear, passes close by Toby and his grouse and Toby must make a decision. He looks at the rabbit and then at Pat, who is throwing sand in what he believes is greyhound speed. Where does duty lie?

So Toby went with Pat but he kept his grouse and the three went across the flat, over the rise far away and were gone, and Bud stood and spoke fervently to himself, to Toby, to Pat and to the jackrabbit, but only I heard him.

The dogs came back, Pat reasoning the chase had been worth whatever was now to happen. Toby no longer had his grouse and he looked confused. Had he done wrong?

"Toby!" stormed Bud. "Where the hell is that bird?"

And now Toby stopped stock still and thought the whole thing out. Did his expression change to one of sudden comprehension? I think it did. He turned and went back the way he had come and when he came back the second time he had the bird. Life is very complicated when a fellow is only eight months old.

Bird hunting is very slow in Alberta this fall.

﷽﷽﷽﷽﷽﷽﷽﷽﷽﷽ Clothes

IT IS MY STUDIED OPINION THAT ANY fisherman who wears a woman's sunbonnet while fishing should be an extremist. He should be extremely small or extremely large. There might be exceptions as in the case of professional boxers or karate experts, but a sunbonnet wearer should be prepared either to defend his choice of headwear or meekly accept what he gets.

Bob Carter qualified for his sunbonnet by being extremely large. Carter, who explained he hadn't been out in the sun much lately and required extra protection, wore his sunbonnet in the most practical manner, snugly tied under his chin. If there is a jaunty way to wear a sunbonnet, Carter didn't bother with it. I had no objection as long as he sat down while we idled the outboard along a rather busy waterfront in a Florida river, but since I was running the boat I preferred that he not stand so it would appear I had a fishing girlfriend a head taller and much wider than I was. Anyone who might know me would automatically assume my pint-sized wife had finally given up on me and was fishing with someone else.

Sunbonnets don't carry the popularity they once did and would be a little difficult to find in most sports shops. Nevertheless, as I watched Bob expertly cast for snook I was at a loss to fault the bonnet. It wasn't in the way, for it was neatly clamped around his head; it certainly didn't admit the sun; and if Stu Apte had been wearing a sunbonnet the other day I couldn't have thrown his headgear into the water with a misdirected streamer fly. For that matter, there is nothing wrong with daisies as male headgear ornaments. They're just a little unusual.

But on the following day Bob didn't wear the sunbonnet, grumbling testily that he didn't think I approved of it, in spite of its efficiency regarding stray lures, sun, mosquitoes and sandflies.

"You just don't like my bonnet," he said accusingly.

He wore a ski mask instead and on the second day he still wore his mukluks, in spite of the fact that the temperature was a close, sticky ninety-something. He had been on duty with the Air Force in Alaska and had noted that mukluks kept the mosquitoes off his ankles. Leave the tops loose, he pointed out, and there was good air circulation in them. I have neither Bob's size nor his commanding bearing, so I wear neither bonnet nor mukluks, but they worked pretty well.

Every outdoorsman I know works on a sartorial image, even if it's just disdain for the things he's expected to wear. Like when you want to ask permission to hunt or fish in a strange land. You're careful not to look too sharp or too crummy, and I once hid Red Monical, my old hunting buddy, because he had some new brush pants that shone and were a little pinkish with bright plastic facings.

I sort of like Western hats because they shed sun and rain but at my age I sure don't want anybody to think I'm playing cowboy so I'm a little cautious until they get good and dirty. Fishing hats are traditionally filthy and there are anglers who wear neckties when they fish but wear hats a garbage collector would walk around. When a beleaguered wife destroys one of those hats, of course, there is a marital crisis, and I suppose such hats have been taken to marriage counselors along with other evidence.

When you wear something new along with strange hunters they tend to watch you very carefully, fearing you don't know how your gun works. I know one deadeye who doesn't look like a real bird hunter at all. He thinks those game bags with suspenders make me look like an unemployed carpenter's apprentice and that a cowboy hat is an insult to the game.

Now at other times he feels jeans are extremely chic, and he has the build for them, but it's different when he goes gunning. Now this guy, who is a little ashamed to be seen with me, wears a shell vest that gleams with cartridges and would be appropriate for a Mexican bandit. He carries a pearl-handled knife almost as long as a cavalry saber and the handle sticks out as if a quick draw might be necessary at any moment.

I hope you are ready for this:

He makes a strong concession to Europe and he wears leather knickers that tend to leave a raw patch on the calf of his leg where his socks have sagged a little above his L.L. Bean boots. Now top this off with one of those Australian hats with the brim snapped up on one side and a tight chinstrap and you should have the picture, believe it or not. Your first impression is wrong because he's an ex-boxer who can walk almost anyone into the ground and shoots his double gun as if a missed bird were a lasting disgrace.

Now, the first time I saw one of those "Florida hats" with the visor in front and the turn-down brim behind I figured it was a sissy arrangement, but it's turned into a real fishing symbol and I get letters from people who want to know where they can buy one. For that matter, I didn't think jumpsuits would catch on with the bass-fishing crowd and that patches advertising Glutz Baits would never be used. But a guy who wouldn't be caught dead with racing stripes or STP stickers on his car will sew stuff on his jumpsuit until he can't bend over and figures epaulet straps are a necessity.

But when I was in the Navy I knew boot sailors who used wire brushes on their white hats to make them look used and buck ensigns who soaked their gold braid in salt water.

Sometimes I feel that I haven't a thing to wear.

Bonefish ⋙⋙⋙⋙⋙⋙⋙⋙⋙⋙⋙⋙

SUDDENLY THE BONEFISH IS THERE and you do not know where he came from.

You have studied the marl bottom, the patches of grass, the sea fans, the small barracuda, the sea urchins, the little sharks and a hundred vague bottom features that might have been bonefish but were not and you have watched well out from the skiff so that there would be room and time to cast. But now the fish is there; no wavering ghost in the shimmering water that always moves from wind or tide, but a big bonefish thirty feet away in a foot of clear depth with the light so perfect you can see the design of his scales and his staring eyes.

You feel huge—like a giant in a giant boat, almost blotting out the sun, and you are sure he sees you and your silly rod, even as you make a floppy cast that causes him to move away at moderate speed or to boil mud and water in a startled flush for the depths. Then you begin to look for another fish.

In these difficult waters bordering the Florida Keys Highway the bonefish can see and feel the speedboats, can watch sunbathers and beachcombers if they wish, and can feel the vibrations of traffic on the bridges. Most of the fish are large, or at least medium-sized, and they have eyed the legs of a thousand waders and almost as many lures.

Farther back from the highway where human traffic is lighter there are flats that see few fishermen and there are less sophisticated fish, more easily moved by boats but more receptive to the fly in some instances, and a fisherman makes those longer trips with anticipation, but after he has seen and caught these slightly easier fish he dreams of shoals of bonefish he has heard of and he knows there are places where bonefish are said to take flies like hungry bluegills. Invariably, he must go and the fish are there as he has imagined.

Perhaps it is somewhere in the Bahamas where the tide runs out between mangrove islands, draining shallows where the gleaming bottom will be bare to the sun when the water is out. And there are the fish, crowding each other so that now and then one of them will lunge irritably on the surface to avoid collision. The skiff is pushed silently by expert hands and the fly goes out, almost at random but aimed where fins and tails are thickest. The strike will not be long in coming, if not on the first cast then on one that comes soon after, and the fish darts off as nearly all bonefish do, the line throwing its little waterspout as the angler lifts his tip and looks for obstructions that may end the contest early. But if the fish escapes there will be another—and another.

At another time the boat is staked at the upcurrent edge of a giant "mud," a milky cloud that spreads constantly in two or three feet of depth, causing the other water to appear especially clear, and a guide releases bits of conch or crab to disappear into the murky section. The fly goes there, and then there is the tentative twitch followed by the lifted rod and a run that may be a little aimless, the fish reluctant to leave the feeding school. And if the boat is used efficiently there may be other fish to come from the same mud.

When his days of this fishing are over the angler goes home, thinking of the fish he has caught, more than he ever caught before, and he is thinking of another trip, perhaps to Central America, where he has heard the bonefish are not only plentiful but very seldom fished. For the moment he wonders if the suspicious residents of the old flat near home can ever again appeal to him.

But he returns to his flat, for it has become a habit, and when he has drifted for a while and then sees a fish he is more excited than ever before. The fish is a long cast away, but this time he is in good position. He is sure it is a bonefish although it appears mainly as a shadow, somehow identified by fractional views of fins and tail, a sort of aquatic abstraction at first. Then he inspects his loose fly line on the boat's deck, an

instant's sharp appraisal, and when he looks back to it the bonefish is easily seen, its head tipped down slightly as it rummages in the thousands of things a bonefish finds on the bottom.

The fish's tail waves gently as it snoops along and behind it are a pair of tiny mud clouds, moving slightly in the tide. When the little pink-and-white fly strikes the water some little distance ahead it makes a tiny plop on the surface, but it is a good cast, and the fish's tail makes a quick move that sends the sleek shape toward the fly, unhurried but purposeful. The head goes down and the fly line seems to vibrate in the fisherman's hand, although the first sign of the strike is simply the stopping of the fly, and then there is the suggestion of a tug as the fish turns slightly and the fisherman fights the desire to jerk hard but manages a quick, sure lift of the rod.

Where the fish has left there is a great swirl of mud and sand and there is the moment of stark fear that the whipping coils of ropelike fly line will catch on something but they do not, and a hundred yards of line and backing feed from the well-tuned reel in a restrained hum. A learned bonefish has been hooked within sight and sound of a swimming party on a nearby beach, and in this case the caster has no wish for wilderness or gullible victims.

The shoals of easier bonefish are far away and the fisherman wants this fish more than any he has ever hooked.

The Bass ›››››››››››››››››››››››››

Cow creek did not run all year. In early summer it was generally broken into isolated pools, partly mud-bottomed and partly rock, lined with willows and weeds and shaded in part by elms.

Its borders were pastureland but the cropland was only a little way back and a good rain always turned the creek chocolate, the eroding wheat and corn fields only partly held by tiling. Contour farming hadn't appeared then. After a rain catfishing might be good. But there were bass in Cow Creek and I had never caught a bass. Don had.

Don had caught his bass, several of them, with an old bamboo casting rod, a Shakespeare casting reel, silk line that he dried meticulously after every use and an Al Foss Shimmy Wiggler with a pork rind that was carefully soaked in brine between trips. When I got my casting outfit it came from Montgomery Ward. The rod was tubular steel and the reel cost ninety-eight cents. I got my plug in town, a Creek Chub Crawdad with rubber legs, and I still have it although the rubber legs have rotted away long since. At first I used silk line but I soon learned crochet thread worked just as well and was much cheaper.

You fished Cow Creek at night, pitch dark or moonlight. That was supposed to be the best time. It never occurred to us to doubt it and it was my first trip that made me a bass fisherman forever. There were three of us, Don, Joe and I, grade-schoolers in straw hats, blue shirts and bib overalls. Joe had an outfit like mine except for the plug, and it is strange I cannot remember his lure, for all else remains so clear—the walk through dust in twilight, the slow cooling of sticky Kansas summer, the clacking scatter of grasshoppers before dark and the fireflies along the creek as night fell. We called them lightning bugs. There was the repeated hoot of a single owl later on and a segment of moon appeared soon after the sun was gone, reflecting from the Rock Hole pool. At its head was only a slow movement of water.

I had learned to cast a little at a farm pond, using a bobber and sinker, but in the dark it was difficult to spread the line evenly on the spool and I thumbed very hard to prevent a backlash, warm spray from the reel touching my face and wetting my hand. Our carbide lamp was left in the grass well back, its light averted from the water but ready for use if tackle needed attention.

We had cast patiently for more than an hour with the attitude of trophy seekers who accept days of failure for a single chance. When the bass struck at my Crawdad plug the lure was somewhere in the black moon shadow of an elm that stood across the creek. I had never heard a fish splash so loudly. I thought then that there was a mighty yank on my rod but now I believe the bass may have missed entirely by either design or accident and that the yank was an imaginary part of what I considered a demonstration of uncontrollable violence. He did not bother my plug again and the three of us stood close together as small boys do in the dark and discussed the attack in hushed excitement.

We went back to our casting and this time a fish took Don's old Shimmy Wiggler and his startled response broke the old bamboo casting rod with a snap like that of a dry cornstalk. Don backed hurriedly up the bank and what he yelled I do not remember but Joe and I dropped our tackle and rushed to help. We grabbed the line and rushed far up through the weeds and when we stopped the fish was forty feet from water. I remember the wet form in the grass, gleaming in moonlight and flopping a little while we cut off any possible return to the creek, and we viewed the precious Wiggler with awe.

Before I slept that night I watched a cooling breeze move the bedroom window curtains in moonlight and I was sure my turn would come soon. I resolved to devote my life to catching largemouth bass.

Grayling ⋙⋙⋙⋙⋙⋙⋙⋙⋙⋙⋙

Until then my grayling had come from smaller water and the broad river seemed unlikely, but Les Allen was confident, slipping his long outboard river boat downstream through the rapids and turning it into a tiny backwater behind a gravel bar to grate it gently against the bank.

"They're right where the water runs over the end of the bar," he said. "Drag your fly through that little ripple."

Lessons hard learned are difficult to ignore, however, and I stood kneedeep an easy cast from the ripple, making the dry fly float down as neatly as I could. It was only after fruitless casts that I accidentally made it drag shamefully and a grayling flashed and slapped at it. That was the way to do it, as Les had said, and when I repeated the performance, the swinging Hendrickson making a little broken vee in the choppy surface, a grayling took and leaped, a delicate fish on delicate tackle, sail fin and iridescence against the backdrop of broad Teslin River and timbered Yukon hills.

We took several fish that way but it would be better, I thought, if the fish would take a dry fly as they are supposed to. Then as the very long north-country summer day went on the sun struck full on the smooth glide of the main river.

"There'll be some insects hatching now," Les said. "Try the main stream."

I turned to the deep water, very clear and very deep, seemingly able to look more than ten feet down, and laid the fly only a short way out where it drifted past, wings cocked and high on the water. The grayling was only a dull moving shadow at first, coming almost straight up, and it became a fish outline without color, then a gleaming thing with broad dorsal, and finally a grayling in full hue that shattered the surface, going up into the air with the fly and falling back to disappear in its own splash, appearing once more as it darted away against the leader's pull.

There were more of them there and in other clean northern waters, but I remember best that one as it came up like a fish spirit which became substance only as it neared the surface.

Cougars ⋙⋙⋙⋙⋙⋙⋙⋙⋙⋙⋙⋙

Bill Matthews hunted a panther he had never seen, trailed it for years with relish and was delighted when he found the cat had been trailing him in turn. But Matthews was a special man who watched the mountains when he talked to you on a Denver street, and if he had been born a hundred years earlier he would have worn buckskin and trapped beaver.

There have been—may still be—human youngsters who grow up with cougars without ever seeing them—and if they are a certain kind of youngster they have learned of their contemporaries through tracks in the snow or the remains of deer or rabbit kills. Matthews was a young hunter when he first began to trail his cougar each fall, and at first he wanted very much to shoot it but in later years he read its tracks for the pleasure it gave him. It was the second year that he found the cat was trailing him as well, the big paw marks very near his boot prints in snow along the rimrock, through the aspen patch and next to the pines on the border of the high sage flat.

So the two of them enjoyed the game for several years and Matthews was not sure what he would do if he ever saw the cat. He often had the feeling that it was watching him and sometimes the trail showed that he was right. He knew the cat's territory and it would take no more than a day or two each fall before he would find its trail. The tracks had become much larger than they had been the first year.

Now, authentic cases of cougars attacking humans are few and far-spaced and dairy bulls have proved a thousand times more dangerous, but there was a day when Matthews became uncomfortable about his acquaintance's intentions. By then it was an old lion.

Matthews had, as before, lost interest in his mule-deer hunting when he crossed the cougar track and he had followed it for more than an hour before lunchtime. Then he sat down where the wind had cleared snow from a rock near a familiar rim and he ate some beef jerky and a piece of chocolate.

When he had rested a few minutes he picked up his rifle and walked a wide circle around his lunch spot to see if the cougar had been watching. He found where it had moved toward him behind cover, its narrow belly leaving a shallow groove in the snow, and he found where it had crouched on a flat boulder, closer than usual, with its feet drawn under it—but what brought Matthews erect and prickled the hairs on his neck was a special mark in the snow. It was where the tip of the cougar's tail had switched gently as it watched him eat his lunch. After that Matthews ate lunch only in broad openings.

Only once have I seen a cougar in the wild when he had not sensed my presence first. It was a mature panther sitting incredibly tall on the edge of heavy timber and he flowed into the bushes so smoothly there was a moment of misgiving as to whether he'd really been there.

There was a time when we rode tired horses along a rocky ridge, eyeing a canyon for sign of the elk which had disappeared into it hours before. We had left a timber trail and only a ragged patch of scrub pines stood on the ridge ahead. Heads down and slogging through patches of snow the horses breathed hard from a climb they had just made and we were about to rest them when they caught a scent from somewhere ahead and became almost unmanageable. It was grizzly country and I fumbled at my saddle scabbard, feeling like an unwilling model for the calendar paintings that have for generations shown rugged horsemen faced by giant humpbacked bruins on narrow mountain trails.

But we saw nothing move and when the horses were calmed we found sections of a cougar's trail where he had passed close by on the way to lower concealment, slipping by through some cat miracle without being seen, somehow using shreds of cover hardly enough to hide a marmot. In the mountains the big cat is a shadow, a wraith and a creature of rumors and tall tales.

We traveled more than a mile of mangrove creek to reach a fishing spot in Everglades National Park—more than a mile of shadowed tunnel, with an idling outboard motor bumping over logs and the boat's bow scraping against mangrove roots and through cobwebs—sure sign the creek had long been unused. It was the same kind of travel that has so often brought us within scant yards of wild turkeys and silent white-tail deer. When the creek opened to a small bay we cut the motor and rowed along the mangrove bank. An unidentified small bird gave alarm calls and a few feet away through the mangroves we heard a series of wheezy coughs, moving far-ther away, and there was one faint shadow drifting briefly and disappearing. Then it was a silent place again.

"An old tom," said the long-time resident. "We woke him up and he was cranky. It's a place a cat could live and if you'll look at a map you'll see why."

Swamps and mountains are better with panthers in them.

⋘How to Give Away a Fish

ANYBODY CAN GIVE AWAY FISH at noon but fishermen don't come home then. Giving away uncleaned fish at ten p.m. takes finesse, salesmanship and foxhole courage.

The objective is obvious, for any fisherman knows reputations are made and kept by giving away dead fish. No neighbor can doubt your ability when the evidence is lying in his sink late at night. These procedures are recommended after many years' observation of advanced practitioners. And even a fisherman who would ordinarily release most of his catch might find he had misjudged and gotten home with too much seafood.

Leaving fish on doorsteps after ringing the bell is the crude approach of a cowardly beginner. Anyone who would do that deserves to keep and clean fish no matter how late and tired he may be. Delivering cleaned fish is simply that—delivering fish—and affords neither challenge nor satisfaction.

The *telephone approach* can be satisfactory when accomplished briskly but can be applied only to fairly close friends.

Like: "Tell Harry to come right over. I want to show him the darnedest thing he ever saw."

Hang up quick. Your friend must drive right over or be a real heel. For all he knows you have a helicopter in the guest room. Once he's there, hand him the fish and ask what it weighs. Note the strategy. Now he has it in his hands. Do this in the living room where he can't put it down without getting slime on something. Step back quickly and make the presentation speech. If he starts to refuse, look hurt.

The *front-door system* is for advanced operators, preferably with house-to-house magazine sales experience. Hold the fish behind you and when the mark answers the bell, hand it to him quickly. By the time he sees he's made a mistake in thanking you, you can be nearly back to your car. This works best very late at night when the subject is not thinking too clearly. Use a very friendly grin, perform the operation with dispatch and try to stay downwind from the subject as the fish may be instantly detected if you caught it early that morning.

It is good to remind some recipients that they requested fish the last time they saw you. Many citizens have received a dishpanful of small, uncleaned bluegills while trying to recall when they asked for fish.

There are highly polished responses to be learned by recipients. One successful politician I know accepts all free fish with fawning gratitude. He doesn't care for seafood but has the fastest-growing rosebushes in town.

When ultimate dexterity has been reached an expert fish giver can look forward to all sorts of good things. I know one man who retired from the field after giving a seven-pound mudfish to a used-car salesman at midnight. Of course he has rare talents and once showed eighty-four snapshots of his children to a stranger in a hotel lobby. I understand he is now a process server in New Jersey.

‹‹‹‹‹‹‹‹‹‹‹‹‹‹‹‹ Long Distance

LONG DISTANCE TELEPHONING is something special to some hunters and fishermen, people who are prone to be a little sentimental anyway.

There was that winter years ago when I called outfitter Garry Vince up in northern British Columbia and the operator asked me if it was in South America, not really so funny a mistake if Colombia comes to mind. Then while the call went through I thought of the thousands of miles between us, miles I'd gone by car, more personal miles than those traveled by air, across the Great Plains where the coyotes still drift along the ridges. I thought of the spine of the Rockies, swathed in snow with high lakes frozen over and the golden trout somewhere underneath the ice. Up Garry's way the bears would be asleep and Garry's packhorses, running wild in the back country, would be wearing off their manes reaching under the evergreen branches to where there would be less snow over the grass. The ptarmigan and snowshoe rabbits would be white and the temperature would be thirty below zero on the glassy Alaskan highway.

In the Yukon a little farther north Les Allen and his smiling Indian wife would be listening to the radio in their cabin and their long outboard river boat would be beached and carefully covered against the rending cold. Their children would be playing quietly as wilderness children can. Outside my window the birds were fussing about the feeder, a gray squirrel was sprawled out on an oak limb soaking up the sun and I'd heard there was some pretty good bass fishing in the St. Johns.

If such communication was awe-inspiring to me, how would it have seemed to my grandfather, the one with the cavalry mustache, who had traveled a part of that land on horseback as he guarded wagon trains? I wished I'd learned more about him when I was a kid.

There was a time when I was stuck in a northern city where the streets were slushy with dirty snow and the world seemed to rumble and roar with traffic. Florida was on the other end of my call and I could imagine the bonefish sliding along the edge of a Keys flat and the blue herons frozen in their patient waiting on a shore of Lake Okeechobee. They came very near for three minutes.

Even in my time the long-distance telephone has been something of a wonder. I remember when I was a cub on a Kansas newspaper and another reporter was making a very long call for those days. Discussing its progress with operators along the way, he covered the mouthpiece with one hand and grinned wonderingly.

"My God, Charley," he said. "That girl is in Arizona."

Last winter I dialed the number of Fred's cabin high in the Montana mountains and when Fred didn't answer I could see the chain tracks where his four-wheel-drive truck had plowed snow down the dirt road toward town. A little below his place the rancher's alfalfa stacks would be white and a hunting golden eagle might be turning over the ridge above Fred's. The mule deer would have come down from the higher country and would be chunky dark-gray spots among the leafless willows in the creek bottom beyond the big woodpile. There might be an elk or two on a wind-scrubbed shoulder of the mountain.

Fred wasn't snowed in that time—or even at home—but I let the phone ring a little while in that faraway cabin and just sat there listening to it and wondering if Fred's bird dog heard it.

I don't know whether Alexander Graham Bell figured on all of this or not.

⋘ The Mangrove Swamp

It is not true that a snook hangs to the mangrove roots with his fins and reaches out for your streamer fly without letting go. And the snook is a pretty fish, I think, if you view from the side. From the front he has a delinquent look, reminding me a little of northern pike or barracuda.

From his bow he looks not at all like a shark but he exudes the same menace when he comes straight for the boat, and when water was clear I have twice seen beginning snook anglers yank plugs away from him and yell, "Damn shark!"

Since he is sometimes derricked from bridges and piers with wire lines and often is trolled up with tackle suitable for marlin, he is low on the social order. He has a name that won't roll in the mouth like "salmon," "trout" or "grayling." His Spanish handle, *robalo*, sounds better, but I've given up on getting anyone to use it.

Go after him with a fly rod and a big streamer or popping bug, up the mangrove creeks where the branches crowd in and the white ibis and anhingas flap off in indignation, and he is a special fish. He lives back where the mangrove roots reach for mud and water, forming a vegetative cave (decorated with captured lures, according to wry snook anglers). Back in the mangrove swamps, miles from open water, you work your skiff gently along the shore and cast against the roots and branches, sometimes a little apprehensive of the swirling turn and the quick slant for cover.

Jim Henely cast twice to the perfect snook pocket and when there was no response he sighed nervously, his lure safely retrieved, and composed a complicated sentence:

"You don't suppose he thinks I don't know he's back there, do you?"

A little later as the water boiled, the flimsy shoreline shook and his line snapped to festoon about Jim's shoulders, I voiced the advice I so wisely offer in such cases:

"Hold him out of the bushes!"

And Jim turned to glare at me.

"Don't just say things like that," he snapped. "*Point* at the bushes. Maybe that would help."

On open water the snook can be different, just another fish, and to me the snook is better when he lives against the roots and old logs in the back country, as he does in much of the tropical and subtropical mangrove belt that circles the world, in places of dark and moody waters where the edges give forth the strange sounds of unseen wildlife, where a touring raccoon stops to stare at your boat and then hand-over-hands along the roots again.

There are great anglers who say only the salmonoids are worthy of their casts. If they will be nice to me, I'll be nice to them.

There are still bald eagles in the mangrove swamps of the brackish Everglades, although not so many now. Twenty years ago it was common to see them high above timbered back-woods bays, riding the thermals or angrily robbing ospreys of choice mullet in plunging air-to-air attacks.

It's National Park water now where we used to hunt widgeon and pintails over a broad bay with a grassy bottom. Eagles live a long time and learn well. I remember one who sat half a mile away from our blind, a white dot on a big buttonwood, and came fast when he heard shooting to race us for a downed duck. He'd probably done it for years. Once, perhaps flustered by our competition, he carried a decoy and its anchor for fifty yards before dropping it in disgust.

There was once when big Ted Smallwood left our blind to race him for a pintail drake, making the little duckboat scoot with his pushpole. With Ted still thirty yards from the bird, the eagle swooped, apparently certain to win the race, but

Ted fired his duck gun in the air and the raider veered off, then came in even lower. Ted fired two shots that time but the eagle towered only momentarily and wheeled back. Ted was reloading and I hoped he wouldn't get too sore.

"Don't shoot too close to him, Ted!" I yelled. "That's our national bird!"

"Yeah," grunted Ted, going back to the pole with a mighty shove, "and he's like the rest of the damned government. Wants everything I've got!"

Armstrong Spring Creek ⟩⟩⟩⟩⟩

Aʀᴍsᴛʀᴏɴɢ sᴘʀɪɴɢ ᴄʀᴇᴇᴋ does not come down from the high mountains that rim Paradise Valley in southern Montana. It rises in a series of cool springs on what's been known as the Armstrong place for a long time. It runs in glides and gentle ripples, under the wooden bridge and past the wooden gate where the faithful park their sleek cars and their battered pickups with tags from every state.

In late summer the underwater vegetation has reached its heaviest growth and long green streamers wave over bottom that is partly stone and partly sand, easily waded for the most part but with deep grooves between the underwater banks of plants, some of which break the surface slightly to make tiny oblong islands. Most fishermen simply call them "moss patches." Warblers, flycatchers, blackbirds and magpies alight on the wet islands and gingerly look for insects.

It is a "creek" in the West, and I insist on the term although I have seen "brooks" that were as large and "rivers" that were as small. It is a home of thoughtful trout, and although there is no other stream just like it, it has many features of eastern America's limestone brooks and England's chalk streams. I have fished Spring Creek for twenty years but I am careful not to pose as a veteran lest I find I am speaking to someone who has fished it for forty years.

Spring Creek is never seen by many of the anglers who work the noisier Yellowstone and hardly note the spot where the creek enters through the cottonwoods; and there are other fishermen who go by foot or horse to the high mountain waters, both steep creeks and cold lakes, that build from nearby melting snow. The trips may be hard but the fish are generally unsophisticated bumpkins that might be scorned by many Spring Creek habitués. So although Spring Creek is less spectacular and may be unknown by some local residents there is a kind of fisherman who prefers the most selective trout and the means necessary to take them. Then Spring Creek is at once famous and a sort of angling back street for careful fishermen who might admit to being snobs.

In such fertile streams the trout population can be amazing. You see that when the hatch is on and the creek's surface becomes a raindrop pattern of rising fish, but if you need more concrete proof you might interview a state biologist who has conducted a census with an electrical shocking machine. *The fish are there.* It is the result of a nearly constant flow of uniform temperature and the insect hatches are often predictable almost to the minute. No fish are planted in Spring Creek and every stone has its miniature colony of water life.

Like the others I park at the wooden gate and walk toward the creek's bank, staying well back lest I throw a shadow across a feeding fish, and if I am not alone I speak softly, for although the cosmopolitan rising trout of Spring Creek have lived with fishermen's voices all summer it is instinctive to approach with stealth.

If I am on time there is little to see on the surface but the curling, swinging spring water itself, the foliage visible below it like flexible green pointers showing the vagaries of the flow. There are delicate murmurs and soft gurgles, but the plop of a shoreline muskrat is heard plainly above them.

The first rise is a silent circle that could have been a gentle boil of current pushed up by some unseen bottom feature, but my attention is tight on the spot now and there is no mistake the second time so I turn toward the car for my waders and tackle, then pause for one last look, and another fish leaves his fleeting mark in another spot. Now the leisurely approach is gone and I fumble hastily with my gear and hurry back to the water, find some regularly rising fish and wade in carefully.

It is eleven a.m. and the action is under way, the quiet dimples almost everywhere with an occasional splash from some small upstart who attacks instead of gulping—or possibly a larger trout jostled by an associate. And when I have selected several prospective targets I maneuver for the right position to show them the fly. The nearer I wade the more complex the nuances of the current appear between my waders and the working trout. And no splashy cast will work, nor will these learned fish consider a fly that drags slightly from current pull on the leader.

There are times when the dimples are caused by fish taking nymphs near the surface, but it is the hatched insects they are after now and I see the new mayflies riding down like tiny sailboats out of control, testing their wings and often disappearing in a trout's lazy circle. Most of them are creamy tan in color today and my fly is a Number 18 Light Cahill on ten feet of leader tapered to 6X, less than two-pound test even without the knots I hope are good. When I have worked out enough line I lay the fly up and across, three feet above where the nearest fish rises regularly. At first the cast appears perfect, but I have misjudged and the fly begins to drag almost instantly as some weaving streak of current pulls on the high-floating line and the little fly plows a furrow in the surface for all to see. My chosen victim pauses for a few seconds to view this angling obscenity but goes back to his feeding as he would have if a thirsty cow had waded past.

I try another fish, an ardent trencherman who does not even return to his holding station between gulps but hangs inches below the surface and takes natural after natural as they parade down. I can see him plainly and get a glimpse of the white lining of his mouth as he turns slightly in his rise. My fly comes down among several real mayflies and he finds it almost above his nose and takes it with a splash.

This one is a rainbow and he jumps high before spurting downstream. He is only a little more than a foot long but smaller fish than that have dived into water growth and broken my tippets. It is satisfying to steer him into open water and then to the surface where he finally hangs on his side in the current, but when I pick him up I know my triumph is

blemished because he had splashed when he took my fly. He
had taken the naturals in gentle dimples, so I know my fly, although lifelike enough to be taken, had not been accepted as a
true imitation. I have not completely won the game.

There are times when the fish take nymphs very near the
surface and the leader is dressed to float down to the last few
inches with an artificial nymph so tiny I have difficulty in tying it on. It is even more difficult than the dry fly for there is
less to see—possibly only a bulge where the fish takes; possibly
only a twitch of the floating leader—and possibly nothing at
all, even after the fraud has been taken and discarded.

So scarce is such treasured water that Trout Unlimited has
leased most of the creek for the public through contributions
of individuals and industrial concerns, so there is a system of
reservations in effect all summer and early fall. When October
comes and most of the fishermen have gone the cottonwoods
are colored gold, the streamside daisies are gone and there is
snow on the mountains that hold Paradise Valley of the Yellowstone. As I approach the creek, transient mallards jump almost straight upward. The muskrats, in evidence all summer
and fall, have a new boldness in their winter preparations and
they try to drive me off with bucktooth disapproval and slapping tails or swim by my waders under water. I can easily see
the bubbles trapped in their fur as they pass.

The magpies cross back and forth regularly, each bird following the same course time after time and observing his territory in detail, ever watching for any of the myriad things a
magpie eats.

Down near where the creek joins the river a beaver lodge
continues to grow, the hub of a dozen drag trails through the
willows. If I pass there before dawn on the way to a duck
blind a beaver may startle me with a disconcerting slap of his
tail on the surface.

And now that most of the fishermen are gone I am more
likely to see the whitetail deer that come silently from the cottonwoods and buffalo-berry bushes to stare at an apparition in

vest and waders, a little stooped in caution as I assess the position of a feeding fish.

Especially in late fall there are the brown and rainbow trout that live in a deep slough feeding so slowly into the main stream that its sluggish motion is hardly noticed. Their surface dimples are even more visible than those of the creek residents and the fish themselves can be seen from the high banks, but there is no way to cast from there because of brush. So I wade by inches into the cold slough, my feet fumbling over boulders and some sunken logs, and then stand perfectly still in hope the slowly cruising trout will accept me as some previously unnoticed and uninteresting bit of half-submerged scenery, the water within inches of my wader tops. Then when I make out a pattern of rises indicating an individual fish's maneuvers I furtively cast an imitation jassid or little nymph and watch the floating leader which I am not above breaking in overenthusiasm.

If a minute goes by and my fish has shown no interest I move my nymph an infinitesimal insect's quiver and wait longer but more often than not I see a quiet bulge somewhere else and know my quarry has moved on.

I have humbly watched better fishermen catch more fish in Spring Creek, and I remember the words of an addict of delicate tackle and difficult trout when told there were much easier ways.

"I don't catch very many," he said, "but they're the only ones I *want* to catch."

Athletes ≫≫≫≫≫≫≫≫≫≫≫≫≫≫≫≫≫≫≫

I HAVE KNOWN SOME BACK-COUNTRY ATHLETES, not always easily picked out from the crowd unless they are on their home grounds. There was the soft-walking detective in Denver who said he had Indian blood and liked to fool around in the mountains. He knew I wrote about the outdoors.

"It might make you a story," he said modestly, "if you'd like to go up there with me during deer season. I'm pretty sure I can bag a muley buck with a knife. If you want to tie in the Indian bit, I guess I could use a hatchet."

I never went but bragging is something I never heard him do.

Nice young fellow was treating the house for termites and he saw a pair of antlers hanging in that cluttered part of the place my wife wryly calls the "office."

He started talking about hunting and I was not too responsive as hunting yarns can get pretty deep around our place and I had to get some work done. I'm afraid I didn't even catch much of his story until he mentioned a rock "about the size of your fist," but then I looked around and saw him better. Big shoulders that sloped down to a narrow waist, a muscled young guy who could move, not very big, maybe 160 pounds.

I swung around in my old swivel chair and asked him if he'd go over that again.

"Well," he said, "I could tell a lot of deer were using this trail and I got this itch to get one without my bow, so I found a big boulder just about the right height and distance and downwind from the trail. And when this buck came along I dived on him and slugged him with that rock. It was a little like bulldogging a steer but he never knew what hit him. I landed right on his neck just above his withers."

134

He began to gather up his tools and acted a little embarrassed.

"I felt kind of funny about it. Kind of crude killing something with your hands like that."

He was at the door and looked back.

"It wasn't a real big buck, though."

Believe him? Hell, yes, I believed him. I sat there for a minute and imagined how he'd gathered himself as his long-gone ancestors might have and how he must have stopped breathing as the buck came alongside. After I heard his truck start I wished I'd gotten his name.

I have admired hunters and fishermen who can walk fast for great distances, day after day—no great feat for athletic youth but sometimes surprising in men who have reached Social Security. For the most part, those older ones are lean and wiry.

There is Roy, who is much older than I but who has walked me into the swampy or rocky ground on several fishing and hunting trips. On a city sidewalk he is a poky dawdler with the foot traffic dividing around him.

"Why do you run me to death in the woods and then spend all day going a few blocks in town?" I asked him.

Roy stared disapprovingly at the city skyline.

"Because sidewalks don't lead anywhere I really want to go," he said.

Retrievers ≫≫≫≫≫≫≫≫≫≫≫≫≫≫≫≫≫≫≫

I DON'T KNOW HOW OR WHY DOGS started bringing things to people.

Now I can understand this pointing business. I figure some old-timer found that his dog made a practice of jumping on game when the game wasn't looking and like a lot of savvy predators he'd stand perfectly still and crouch until the right moment came. Then he'd jump. Well, the old boy who owned this wolfy-looking specimen probably figured that if Rover would delay his spring for just a little bit it would give him a chance to flatten the bird or rabbit with his club, or possibly throw a grass net over an entire covey.

Now I don't know how he persuaded Rover to stand still for a little extra time. Maybe he turned him for a couple of flip-flops with a vine around his neck when Rover made his play. It may be that he even bonged his helper with a club every time his best friend dived at a ruffed grouse. Anyway, dogs learned to point or set game, and I like to think it was earlier than most historians believe. I like to think of Uglug and Zog sitting around a fire and Uglug telling Zog that others could have all of the close workers they wanted but that Uglug liked big-going dogs that worked two spear throws out into the prairie.

Now setters learned to hunker way down so a net thrower could make a productive toss and that's natural for somebody who's getting ready to jump anyway. It took quite a while be-fore hunters decided a pointing dog should stop squatting down, and old Rover's descendants had to go through quite a program. The old hunting prints and even the photographs and paintings of forty or fifty years ago show pointing dogs pretty well flattened out and with their tails sticking straight back, but somebody decided pointing dogs should stand erect with their tails and heads high. This makes them easy to see but I sort of liked the old-fashioned way because those dogs looked as if they were really tending to business and a dog standing straight up just doesn't prepare me for what's going to fly up my shirt front.

Anyway, it has been so long since pointers got the idea that even they don't know how it all started. Because of all that breeding even a bumble-footed puppy might point almost anything he can see over his dish, and that is instinctive. It would be insulting to infer that old McGillicuddy is acting on instinct when he points a cock pheasant, waits for you to come up and then jumps in the air to make the bird fly instead of run.

It would be a cheap shot to say it is instinct for an English setter named Ralph to slip around to head off and stop a bunch of bobwhites legging it through the wire grass in south Georgia and then point back toward the people with guns. If Ralph didn't figure that out, his instincts sure are complicated.

So I don't worry much about pointing but I don't know why some dogs want to retrieve, and I figure that if any psychologist wants to explore some real canine hangups he should study retrieving. If he can stay off his own couch long enough he should have dog dope to make Pavlov a piker.

Now there was this retriever field trial and the event called for a gunshot fired on the bank, whereupon a couple of guys sitting in an anchored rowboat would toss out a live mallard duck with its wings and legs suitably trussed. When a dog got the signal after an appropriate period to test his steadiness, he'd hit the water, get the disgusted mallard and bring it to his handler under the nitpicking eyes of the judges.

This big Lab had been there a lot of times before and he looked like a winner, sitting there with the muscles all lumped up under his shiny coat. His head was straight forward but if he missed any part of the setup it wasn't important.

The gun was fired and one of the men in the boat chucked out the mallard but that duck knew his way and his feet came loose so he went back toward the skiff like a speedboat about to get up on plane. He sculled around the boat out of sight of the gallery and he found a hiding spot up against the hull on the side opposite where he was dunked and out of sight of the Lab.

I guess the rules were a little vague about that kind of performance. Anyway, when the handler blew his whistle that dog hit the water so far from shore you'd wonder if he knew how to swim. But he could swim all right—about like an oversized otter. He was at the spot where the duck had splashed down before you could say, "Lookit him go!" Then he rose up high in the water to look around and he shot a glance back at his boss. No help there. Then he headed for the boat where the duck smells came from. He went out of sight for a few seconds while he looked for his duck and then the skiff keeled over a little on his side. It began to swing around a little too.

"Wait a minute!" one of the men said, and the other man said, "Watch it!"

There was this big, black head over the gunwale and a lot of big white teeth and quite a few splinters. He had him a whole crate of ducks and one of the men grabbed it just before he hauled it over the side. Then the dog decided one duck would be enough and he started taking the crate apart. More splinters. His handler was running up and down on shore and trying to figure an appropriate signal and the men in the boat were discussing the problem with the Lab. They were not giving him orders; they were appealing to his sense of fair play.

So he tried to tow in the boat and found it was anchored. Finally, he went back to shore and glared at the gallery before shaking himself.

I went hunting with Luke and Ed down in north Florida. Ed said Luke was a well-trained quail pointer he'd just bought for considerable money and that he'd already proved he was a fine retriever by bringing in sticks from the back yard.

Luke kept whining and yipping a little in the back of the

station wagon on the way out, evidently knowing where we were going. We went a few miles out of town and turned into a sand road through palmettos and sand pines to a secret place where Ed said the quail population had exploded. When he opened the tailgate Luke came out of there reaching for the ground and he was past the second palmetto patch before Ed could say *unload*. It didn't take Luke long to wind birds and he was stylish enough for a calendar artist. He came down on those bobwhites with head and tail up and he had that look of being there for the rest of the day if necessary.

Ed looked as if he'd just struck oil and stood and beamed for a minute before walking up. There were only a couple of birds and one of them burned off toward some heavy cover while the other cut off high on Ed's side. My bird was a pretty easy shot and I got him center. He end-over-ended into a clump of palmettos and Luke was after him before he hit the ground. He left the palmettos shaking where he went in fast but he didn't come out right away, and Ed, who had marked *his* bird down, didn't want to move, so he said maybe I'd better check on the dog as he sure wouldn't want him to get hit by a snake.

I went into the palmettos but I didn't have to go very far. There in a small opening was Luke with a happy look on his face and some small feathers at the corners of his mouth. There were three or four more on the ground. He gave a re-fined burp and then roared off to look for Ed's bird.

"Did he find yours?" Ed yelled. I told Ed he sure had. Luke ate Ed's bird too and Ed asked me what I thought he should do. I was very careful not to say what I *felt* like doing but I was flattered that Ed should ask me about dog training. On the way back to the station wagon we went through some swampy ground and Ed got his feet wet.

"I've got some dry socks here in the car," he said. "I don't want to drive home with wet feet."

So he sat down on the tailgate and took off his snake leg-gings and boots while Luke sat and watched. Then he took off one sock and dropped it on the ground. Luke leaned over and went *gulp* and the sock was gone. Luke looked expectantly at the other boot.

"You know," Ed said, "I don't believe I ever can break that dog of eating birds."

Jack Bannon and Johnny Bragg sent back a beautiful pointer they had on trial. It pointed beautifully and hunted dead perfectly but it ate big pieces of birds.

"We shouldn't have sent him back," Jack said sadly. "We should have had his teeth pulled and bought him dentures. Then we could have taken his teeth away when he hunted."

Now old McGillicuddy is one of those spectacular retrievers that you don't want to put down on the second day of pheasant season if there have been a lot of hunters out because he's likely to bring in your limit of lost birds before you can get any shooting at all. He's a freckled Brittany who keeps his hand in by bringing you old bones and stuff if there's been very little shooting. Accept his offering and he'll zoom right back to his normal casting range and get to hunting again. But McGillie doesn't like discord and if some other dog argues with him about who's going to retrieve, McGillie will not only give him the bird but he'll retire from that department. He'll continue to point but every time you shoot McGillie will hide and let the other dog do the fetching.

McGillicuddy's chief problem is proper distribution of dead birds, figuring shooters should come out even at the end of the day. He is adamant about this and even the pleading of his owner, Ben Williams, doesn't change the procedure. McGillie never considered Ben as his owner anyway, but more of a business associate and kennel flunky.

McGillie loves to hunt ducks, even though his coat wasn't intended for a river full of slush ice. He knows, of course, when it's a duck-hunting trip. In fact he sometimes arranges a duck hunt and when you're jump-shooting along a creek or river he doesn't range at all, just follows along with no corny

commands such as *heel*. If you get down to crawl up on a good spot, McGillie sits down and waits until you shoot, and I think he could find a dead teal sealed in plastic and buried in mud. Some years back Ben shot a big Canada goose over some cold, swift water and McGillie had trouble getting ashore with it. In fact, weighing in at thirty-five pounds, McGillie and the goose docked some two hundred yards downstream. He then crossed geese off his retrieving list, refused to look at them or sniff them, and when Ben puts one in the car McGillie crowds to the farthest corner he can reach and averts his eyes.

But ducks are different and McGillie feels they should be distributed equally among gunners. Ben and I sneaked along this little creek, having spotted a bunch of mallards. But when we stood up expecting them to take off about the same distance from each of us we found they had moved and I couldn't see them at all for a patch of willows. Ben knocked down two—one in the water and one out in some tall grass in a boggy area. It was a long shot and to get near the birds Ben had to walk downstream to find a crossover. McGillicuddy had seen none of the action but he crossed over with Ben, retrieved the bird from the water and delivered it with his version of style—a kind of prance with his eyes popped out and rolled down to see the ground over the duck.

Then he went out into the marsh and got the other big mallard drake. It hadn't come down immediately and it was quite a trip but you could see his progress in moving grass and an occasional orange spot on white. He came in from his trip and straight toward Ben who said, "Attaboy, McGillie. Good dog!"

Then Ben reached for the duck but McGillie sidestepped him and headed for the creek, slogging through mud and weeds and floundering in places since he's no Labrador, while Ben said something about "you crummy little varmint!"

And when McGillie reached the creek he slopped along the bank, his head up to keep the mallard's wings from dragging and the whites of his eyes showing as he tried to see the mud ahead of him. He went up to a narrow place and swam across, scratched and floundered up the other bank, looked around for me and saw me another fifty yards away just standing there gawking. He brought the mallard to me, thumped it down on the ground and said something that sounded like "Whew!" Then he went back across the creek to find where Ben wanted to hunt next.

But then, McGillie is a personality. He is sometimes a little furtive and Ben thinks he would be a pickpocket if he were human. There was the time he ate the ham that had been left on the kitchen counter. But he put the bone back on the platter.

Now Kelly, another Brittany, was a terrible retriever—wonderful hunter for dead or crippled birds but an unconventional fetcher. He gave up classic retrieving early in life on a snowy day when Max Stevenson and I waited for him to bring a dead Hun up a steep hill. Kelly came up the hill and laboriously crawled under a fence, started toward me and then toward Max. He was tired and muddy but wanted to hunt instead of carrying birds around. He stopped and thought for a moment, spat out the bird (ptooie!) and retired from formal retrieving forever.

Oh, yes, I tried all of the book methods but he acted as if he'd read the books too and thought the whole thing was silly. He'd carry a bird through anything until he was sure I saw it and then he'd throw it down.

Before I gave up on him there was a time in pheasant country when he dragged a bird out of some heavy brush after I'd thought it was lost forever. He threw it down and a few minutes later I dumped a big rooster on a bare hillside where it stood out like a crashed bomber on a lawn. For training purposes I whistled him from across a creek and said, "Fetch."

Kelly looked around and saw the rooster, trotted up to within ten feet of it, made sure it wasn't going anywhere and then gave me a long look of disdain, turned and went on about his hunting. His reasoning was that I might be clumsy and stupid about finding downed game but that I had hands and he didn't, and even a human could see *that* bird.

He decided early in life not to carry a live pheasant rooster, since they have spurs. He pursued cripples in a wild, head-long, brush-smashing rush but I wondered for a while why all of them came in dead although he wasn't hard-mouthed. At first I thought he always made a stop to get a better hold. He broke their necks.

Kelly knew there were birds I could not follow and there was the time in Alaska when he plunged over the cliff and went down into a misty depth in a rattle of stones after a falling ptarmigan. I looked over the edge in horror to see a little dog with a dead bird coming back up in gasping, clawing mountaineering. He dropped it at my feet but refused to bring any ptarmigan I could get to myself.

I must confess that pheasants were not the only cripples Kelly zapped. A sage grouse is a big bird and a rooster might weigh seven pounds. Sometimes they won't hold for a dog and they take off across their enormous land like underpowered airliners.

Kelly pointed a big one and it flushed wild, clattering up a long slope, and I thought it was out of range but Max Stevenson pushed his old pumpgun and his duck load whanged. Apparently the bird was addled but not too hard hit and it landed in a bare spot on the hilltop where it drew itself to its full height and looked around in plain view. Kelly was on his way, but fresh from woodcock and quail, he was not prepared for such an apparition—a two-foot-high bird seemingly standing its ground—and he slid to a stop four feet away. An instant of stalemate and then he crouched, circled a little and charged in an explosion of feathers.

In warm weather, which was always hard on Kelly and his all-out hunting methods, he took brief rests at water holes. Across a brushy draw Red Monical winged a cock pheasant that struck the ground with his feet already churning and went scooting into the brush.

"Get 'em, Kelly!" Red yelled, and I saw Kelly coming from somewhere in a brindle streak and into the brush with a crashing noise. There were smashing sounds for a few moments and then dead silence. Red looked around in there but found nothing and I suddenly suspected there might be water at the bottom of that big draw. So I went stumbling, cursing and whistling through the brambles, then falling among the cattails, and there was what I suspected. At the very bottom was a muddy puddle of smelly water and in the exact center of it was Kelly, on his belly, his legs spread-eagled and his tongue lolled in satisfaction at the cool sensation.

"You stinking rodent," I said. "Where the hell is that rooster?"

And as if he wondered what all of the fuss was about, Kelly reached down *under* himself in that muddy mess and brought out a slimy thing shaped exactly like the beautiful cock pheasant. He dropped it where I'd have to wade for it and sprinted off to resume hunting.

When it was hot and no water was present, Kelly dug holes, and our favorite quail territory looked like an old battlefield. He'd dig five minutes to arrange a cool hole for a one-minute rest, and a kill usually meant a break—end of one phase and a respite before beginning of another.

Up went the bobwhites and I caught one at the top of its climb over the hedge. It fell clean and trailing a pair of feathers, going into a patch of weeds—and Kelly had been watching the other birds. When I told him to hunt dead he went about it in his usual efficient manner with vacuum-sweeper sounds and careful quartering—then disappeared through some dog fennel and somewhere in the right direction. Silence.

I didn't whistle or call. I went softly after him and listened for a panting dog. I heard it and approached the scene. There was Kelly in a masterpiece of pit construction, on his cooling belly, legs stretched out behind. On the rim of his hole lay a bobwhite, feathers unruffled.

"Fetch!" I said, a word without meaning any more but an accepted formality.

Kelly carefully placed his nose under the quail and flipped it for a few inches to make sure I saw it. Then he stared off in the other direction. I knew then I was being trained. The smug little wretch!

‹‹‹‹‹‹‹‹‹‹‹‹‹‹‹Old Ridgepoles

THE NUMBER OF OLD MAPS has increased through the years, not because I consciously collect them but because I have never thrown one away, always telling myself that I'll go back someday and need them. Most of them are topographic maps of fishing and hunting country, but there are some old charts of the southwest Florida mangrove coast, drawn from aerial photographs taken back in the twenties—large-scale and more helpful to a small-boat man than modern Coast Guard charts. The old ones are still printed. And there are some ordinary road maps with penciled directions and added lines that usually end with X's some distance from any road. I've forgotten what some of them mean.

Some of the old topo maps have been cut and pieced together with transparent tape to show a penciled route that crosses a break between two large sheets which were too troublesome to take along. Some are dirty wth memorable stains from flattened peanut butter sandwiches, rain and snow, and if you check very closely you may even detect a trace of woodsmoke smell.

There is one map, dogeared, wrinkled and patched with tape at the folds, that carries a short note from years ago. It says:

"The elk went over into Skunk Creek. Mike."

Mike's real name is Mary Ann and the note is in an uncertain scrawl because she wrote it with the soft lead tip of a .270 cartridge. That was the fall when winter was early and only a trickle of water came through the icy little creek by camp. When Mike's husband Bud was alive we really hunted for fun and nobody was worried about the elk dropping over into Skunk Creek, least of all Mike, who had trailed them until dark after leaving the note near camp.

Before the Forest Service road it was a long trip to that camp and you had to feel out your route with a four-wheel-drive rig. Then you walked into higher country and anything you killed came out the hard way.

I cut the ridgepole the first time my wife Debie and I found the spot. We went in two days before the season opened. We followed a good jeep trail across open pasture, grass and sage, and we stopped when we saw a big badger watching us from his hole thirty yards away. When we stopped he ducked his head but curiosity overcame caution and he popped up again, then back down, then up again, and kept that up in a ridiculous jack-in-the-box routine for some time.

We passed the old homestead which may have been the sad end of someone's dreams—but could have been the start for a prosperous rancher who moved out to the highway—and we forded the marshy area. We went through there very cautiously but with momentum, our little engine winding busily. Another year I was to mire helplessly in that spot and Red Monical and I worked for hours with a come-along and deadmen to get to dry ground.

But it was a dry year when Debie and I crossed and we got into higher country, sage hills with aspen patches in the draws, and we worked our way on old trails until we were very near the base of some real mountains with fringes of rimrock, heavy pine forests, grassy parks and a jumble of ragged rock formations on top—they show red in the sunset.

It was there that the topo map became confusing and I am still not sure of the name of the creek where I cut the ridgepole. A mile from where we stopped we pushed four muley bucks from a clump of evergreens, the biggest one at the rear, and they bounced upward for a hundred yards, stopped to look back, and then disappeared over a ridge.

We made the camp beside a stand of aspens and thirty feet from the cold brook which was to lull us to sleep so many times. I cut the ridgepole with a little cruiser's axe and it went up easily between two slender trees, holding our white wall tent solid. The tent became dingy through the years and was finally cut into small tarpaulins when we got something more modern. We still use those tarps when we carry bird dogs on the car seat or need something to sit on when the ground is wet. We call them "pieces of the old tent."

That first evening a little forkhorned buck watched me drive the tent stakes and a doe with two fawns decided we were harmless and fed on one of the sage foothills three hundred yards away. That night after the wind turned chill a coyote called from very close by. First he sang a high-pitched wail and then he broke it up and played it back to us in little pieces.

At dawn we slipped up to a rise and mounted a spotting scope. We saw a big bull elk with two lesser bulls far up the slope and they grazed for an hour before disappearing in a wrinkle of the mountain. It was farther than it seemed, as I learned the next morning when the season opened and I panted my way up there. I went up in darkness and heavy fog concealed any game that might have been present. But later in the day when I perched on a high knob two Shiras moose were great dark figures in the binoculars, feeding about a swampy seep higher up. And from the same spot I saw bighorn sheep, almost in the crags and so far away I could not make out horns at all.

From a park high up the mountain the pattern of our creek and others was visible. There were beaver ponds above and below us and early in hunting season before they froze there were mallards on them. Later on that year when we came back to our campsite and lifted the ridgepole again there was snow and our gasoline lantern glowed in a wide circle on the sage slopes about us. One night a flock of snow geese, probing for some lost mountain pass, swung above us for hours and it was a long while before we realized our pond of light was confusing them. When the lantern went out the musical calls changed slightly and then faded for good. I remember most of the places I have heard geese or coyotes.

There was one year when I skirted an edge of timber, a two-hour climb from camp, walking just inside the trees and moving upwind when I saw a red shirt ahead and met a stranger, a young, hard man with scarred boots and the heavy wool pants of a cold-weather hunter. His rifle sling was slick with use and the rifle itself carried curly walnut, a touch of engraving and signs of careful wear.

I offered jerky, he offered a smoke, and we sat against a boulder to look across fifty miles to another range and saw one tiny reflection that must have come from a valley ranch window or a stock tank.

"A year ago," he said, "I killed a bull right over here in that little park."

"I had a spotting scope and I saw you dress it out from over across the canyon," I said.

So we sat and grinned at each other and never bothered to mention where we had been in the intervening twelve months. Instead, we talked of rifles, cartridges and mountain boots, how the deer had disappeared since the day before the season opened, and how there were more hunters each year. Nice fellow.

The second year at our camp the ridgepole was ready to use and I don't know why I was surprised to find it still there. Af-

ter that, I expected it each time. The second year there was
no sign a human had been there since elk season but a tin can
had been dug from our old garbage pit, probably by a coyote,
so I made the pit deeper. There were a few sticks of firewood
we hadn't needed. We used a sheet-iron stove and when it was
almost zero outside the tent it could be very cold inside just
before dawn after the fire had burned down. It would have
held to a smolder with the draft turned down and I'd hump
over to it in my down mummy bag like a chilled caterpillar,
open the draft, give it a few pokes and add a couple of sticks.
Then the stove would roar for a few minutes and getting up
wouldn't be bad at all.

There was one year when I caught the flu—or something—
on opening day. Anyway, I was up in some rock spines that
stuck out of the mountain like the curved backs of giant dino-
saurs and gave a good view of half a dozen game trails. I knew
there were hunters above me but I heard only early-morning
bird noises and the dull, re-echoed boom of a rifle on somebody else's mountain. I had a touch of fever and all of the
aches that go with my annual flu bout so I just sat down and
waited where the sun struck my neck. Below me the timber
thinned to strands following creeks and arroyos downward
into grasslands.

An elk can move like a fading shadow in thick timber but
when elk forego caution they can crash and clatter like a cavalry charge and someone above me had sent a band downhill
at a noisy run. They stopped at the forest edge just above me
and changed tactics to a quiet march along the timber's
edge—mostly cows and calves but with one butter-fat spike
bull. It was the spike I chose and I slipped the safety forward,
my left arm in a dead rest atop the stone, and when the spike
stopped to look back the way he had come the crosshairs settled behind his shoulder only 175 yards away.

As my finger took up on the trigger I thought of the labor of
dressing him out—best to quarter him immediately in such
warm weather—and of the mighty effort of getting him across

and down the ridges toward camp. My back was hurting and my head ached and my trigger finger paused. I knew I had a bit of fever and I didn't know how to get help, so my finger slacked and before I had really decided the bull dissolved in sage and pine. Then I heard nothing but bird noises and a jeep grinding up a steep pitch miles away somewhere. I stretched out in the sun for an hour and then trudged slowly back to camp where I was sick for three days, giddy with fever, and a difficult sleeping-bag patient for Debie, who finally got me down out of there with the help of another hunter. I killed no elk that year.

There was once when I really had a big bull cornered, I thought. I saw him coming down the mountain, half a mile away, and he went into a small patch of timber, hardly two hundred yards across. In there, I thought, I'd trail him carefully and find him frozen stock still with his antlers merging into dead branches. First, I thought, I'd see his long legs among the trees, and then I'd pick out the shadowy rest of him.

The tracks were there, big, round-toed and a little splayed with his weight, and they followed a well-used trail but there was less snow back where the pines grew thick and there had been other elk there. So I moved slowly with long pauses and the pine needles were quieter than crusty snow. Once I heard a hysterical pine squirrel up ahead, undoubtedly directing his invective at the quarry, and when I'd doubled back two or three times I thought there was a slow-moving shadow beyond a thicket. Once a stick cracked loudly and I stood staring in that direction for five minutes but nothing moved. I walked that way and found nothing.

I had been in the miniature forest for more than an hour when the bull tired of the game and broke out into the open to race off to better hiding. I heard the receding hammering of his hooves but I never saw him leave.

There were big bucks near our camp and as muley bucks do elsewhere they became scarce each year just after the season opened, but go back in there when the snow had come and the beaver ponds were frozen and you might find one of the "old men of the mountain" with his little bunch of does. That would be about the second week of November in most years.

Generally there were no more than two or three hunters in our camp but the year Red Monical killed his big buck there were several of us, and on that morning Red, Jack Ward and I were making a circuitous move on the mountain's shoulder, hoping to have elk pushed to us from other members of the party.

We saw the deer across a wide draw, a buck and doe moving with purpose and looking backward at intervals toward invisible hunters they had scented or seen. They were about to enter timber. I was thinking elk and it was no deer hunt but Jack said, "Bust him, Red! He's a big one."

And Red sat down hard, his elbows groping for his knees because it was a long, quick shot, and his .257 Weatherby banged just once.

The taxidermist did his work well and the big shoulder mount pushes out of the wall where Red can see it while he works. Every year I stand and look at it for a few moments and remember the morning sun on the mountain snow, the steam from our little creek and the ruffed grouse who used to puff his chest and glare at us as we came down through the willows just above camp.

The ridgepole changed a little through the years. The bark came off and it was shiny where the ropes went at the ends. It may be just a rotten stick now. The Forest Service road went in and I haven't been back for a long time.

The Chum Line >>>>>>>>>>>>>>

Off Bermuda the chum line is a sparkling, wavering path in the dark-blue water, streaming astern of the anchored cruiser, appearing more like a trail of sequins than simply handfuls of tiny baitfish scattered from the transom.

Farther down and invisible to the anglers is another line of chum, released from a weighted chum basket in the depths, and all moving with the tide, carefully appraised by the captain, who has chosen his spot with care and fathometer.

Bermuda is a low mound on the horizon, its buildings visible as white specks when the light is right. At early morning the sportfisherman had left the harbor where the white sand bottom made the water green and where the channels showed plainly as darker strips. Bright flowers splotched the hills that hemmed the anchorage and the sputter of Bermuda's little motorbikes was finally drowned by the diesel's mutter. On the way out there were rock cliffs and the cruiser slid confidently between underwater boulders, some of them almost awash in the troughs of inshore swells. The hazards were brown and ominous by day and in some of those areas the boats would not move at night.

The offshore chum is a sort of party line of the depths and almost anything can appear in it. There may be small fish to flash at the slowly sinking particles that extend steadily from their apex, and there may be larger fish who seek not so much the chum itself as the fish that come to take it, and just how far the sight and odors of his offering may extend, not even the captain knows. He probes a great swatch of ocean.

There is almost a picket fence of rods in the cockpit—light spinning tackle, fly rods and heavier stuff to match anything that appears, for the chum fisherman is an opportunist.

The robins arrive, small hurrying fish that dart into view as

a compact school and then become scattered as each fish takes its own direction for a particular tidbit, and fishermen cast small lures, flies or baits at them, each angler jokingly proclaiming his skills as a fish catcher. The robins leave except for half a dozen that have been caught and will be turned into chum for something bigger.

Then someone's rod dips more urgently and the first blackfin tuna is on although he has not been visible in the chum. Staring hard down into the sea a visiting fisherman is more than ever aware of what swims unseen below the glittering baitfish, and while the tuna fighter calls for a rod belt someone else has hooked something heavy and slow-moving down there.

Not all of the visitors are welcome. There is the barracuda which appears well astern, an ominous, cigar-shaped shadow several feet long and moving in and out of the line to disappear with an apprehensive promise by the mate that he would be back. When he does come back it is with a rush and someone's yellowtail snapper is reduced to nothing more than a hooked head, but there is special tackle rigged for the "barrie" and when he finally loses all caution to chase a huge bait along the transom he is impaled on a big gaff before he has so much as touched his objective. Then the fishing goes on.

Yellowfin tuna are prizes of this fishing—hard-charging fish which sometimes hang hungrily in groups and are hooked on both bait and artificials, their colorful beauty enhanced by the sea's dark-blue background and the flowing distortion of the ever-moving surface.

And I have to admire the wahoo especially. Perhaps it is the knowledge that he is a traveler, that he goes at great speed and crosses more ocean than any sedentary bottom dweller. Partly it is his appearance, streamlined and striped, and undoubtedly it is his habit of appearing in a sweep of inspection to disappear for some time and to come by again with the impression that he has gone a long way and seen many things in the few minutes since his last visit.

There was one that appeared, first as a suspicious shopper

sliding effortlessly through the chum far back, and then as a businesslike feeder, fairly deep but easily seen, turning swiftly in constant motion and then disappearing completely for several minutes.

Then he came back, barely beneath the surface, this time ignoring the boat and the ogling fishermen to cross and recross the chum, and I somehow put a bait where he wanted it and heard the line hiss as he made his circling run, suddenly much farther out than I could believe. Then I stumbled toward the bow with the rod clutched awkwardly as I climbed past the outriggers and reached for handholds to keep him from fouling the anchor line, which he did anyway, although we somehow landed him despite my inept fumbling.

But the part I remember best is the little mound of Bermuda on the horizon, the glittering jewels of chum in the gentle blue-black swells and the lean wahoo appearing from nowhere, tiger-striped and seeming to have slowed only briefly from his endless travels of the Atlantic.

Baitimademyself >>>>>>>>>>>>

IF YOU'LL CHANGE A MANUFACTURER'S LURE just a little you'll derive a lot more satisfaction from your catch. The personal pride in using a Baitimademyself is Number One incentive for a lot of fishermen. The phrase is used enough that I now recognize it as a single word.

Taking off or adding a treble hook is strictly bush-league stuff for timid souls with little initiative. A real bait changer has the paint pot out before he opens the new plastic box and will tell you the purple polka dots he puts on the tail are the difference between filling the stringer and eating hamburger.

He will judiciously bend the lip of a time-honored bass plug or even scrape off all the factory paint and start over after adding weight at the nose or taking it off at the tail. He will change the location of the line connection and remove the eyes if there are any. If there are no eyes he'll install some. If the original eyes won't come off easily, he'll paint circles around them.

After doing these things he may add a string of metal beads, a couple of spinners, a plastic skirt and a weed guard. Any fish he catches on the finished product is landed in defiance of the folks who made the original. He pays a high water bill for testing his alterations in the bathtub and some of his products are a little extreme. One guy made a plug especially for night fishing but never tested it. He was afraid of it after dark.

After using the altered lures for a while the fisherman manages to forget he ever bought them in the first place and takes full credit for the creations. Then as the years go by he may work gradually back toward the original form and will swear the first manufacturer stole his ideas.

Although special black-bass models may not catch quite as

many fish as the originals they have a lot of advantages in mystifying the opposition.

Suppose you've just caught a big string of bass on a Hawaiian Wiggler and you show them to another fisherman.

"What are you using?" he yells.

"Baitimademyself," you reply, leaving him completely in the dark and keeping yourself honest because you did trim three strands from the wiggler's rubber skirt. This guy will take the registration number of your boat and report that he has encountered an unsung giant of the fishing game.

Catching fish on something not originally intended for fish catching will mark you as a muddy-footed genius. If you can produce with a tie clasp or can opener you will be almost as famous as if you had done it by mutilating some manufacturer's carefully designed plug, and I know one sport who gained renown through the efficiency of his cardboard lures. They didn't last long but they certainly were baits he made himself—with scissors.

But the lure doctor is an amateur beside the fly fisherman. The standard trout and bass patterns of years gone by are completely buried beneath thousands of variations and creations with exotic names such as Purple People Eater and Spuddler (a cross between a muddler and a spruce fly and pretty scary). After struggling with bundles of hair, feathers and thread for months and trying desperately to come up with a fitting name for his finished product, one tier glanced in an illustrated book and found his creation was simply a Silver Doctor streamer. He'd come full circle.

Anybody who makes a fly out of simple things such as chicken feathers or bucktail is a piscatorial square, and if you can't use Tasmanian monkey hair, polar bear or unborn calf you may as well buy your flies. I have a personal feeling that the biggest hazard to our thirty-some whooping cranes is the possibility some fly-tier might decide he needs their feathers.

For some time my neighbor was the envy of all when his

productive weakfish streamer featured "Pogo hair," sought diligently by his friends in all sorts of supply catalogs. It finally came out that Pogo was his yellow-tinted mongrel dog—but only after crew-cut Pogo had gone to his reward.

But if you want to impress other fishermen, concentrate on seemingly minor changes and be adamant about them. I still recall with awe the California trout fisherman who explained that the secret of his success was the length of the red tag ("tail" to you bait fishermen) on a black wet fly he was using. He bought these flies by the dozen and the tail was an eighth of an inch long on the commercial product. Using manicuring scissors, he would meticulously cut a sixteenth of an inch from the tail and go forth in confidence. Since he was a good fisherman he had a lot of imitators, some of whom decided a thirty-second of an inch was a more effective amputation, but I can't say it was ever proved conclusively.

Custom fly-tiers get long-distance calls and registered mail calling for urgent changes in standard patterns, and once these changes are made customers are likely to change the name. For example: An eager-beaver brown-trout seeker calls a custom fly shop and orders two dozen size 16 Light Cahill dry flies but he wants them to have blue-dun tails. The girls at the tying bench shrug their shoulders and tie 'em up, little realizing they are on the threshold of history.

A year later they get another order from a brand-new client who wants a dozen Hogglesneimer Choices in size 16. Since this is a new one on the girls they ask for a sample and—you guessed it—it's the Light Cahill with the blue-dun tail and the new customer is a little perturbed that they never heard of it when Mr. Hogglesneimer recommends it so heartily.

But to be serious for a moment, do you know how to tie the Waterman Weasel?

Live Decoys ⇉⇉⇉⇉⇉⇉⇉⇉⇉⇉⇉⇉⇉⇉

You youngsters who never hunted ducks with live decoys have missed a whole bunch. Some of you probably think all mallards are alike without much personality and you've wasted the slow hunting days watching factory imitations bobbing stupidly in front of a blind. Before live decoys became illegal you could have devoted all of that time to scientific observation of individuals like Pete and Repeat.

Pete was an English call duck and was a little small, even for that lightweight breed. You wanted little ducks because they didn't take up much space and were easy to carry in a burlap sack. I had ten cents invested in Pete, having won him at a turkey shoot. At those events in our farm country the turkeys were won by shooting shotguns at stationary marks and the most shot pellets in a given area would win a turkey, or you might just shoot at a little cross and whoever got a pellet nearest the center was a winner.

But it cost more money to shoot a shotgun and there would be a crate of ducks for .22 rifle shooters. The impresarios of the event would furnish the rifle with open sights and you paid a dime to shoot at an X on a piece of paper. Whoever came closest to the center won a duck. Ten entrants would give a good profit to the management because the ducks cost twenty-five cents to fifty cents on the open market.

When I won Pete the crate was filled with little mallards provided by someone who raised them as decoys. I stood up offhand like everybody else and when they'd brought in the little paper squares it developed that I'd cut the center out of the X. That was sheer luck because with all of those people watching it's a wonder I hit the paper.

I got the rest of my decoy contingent at around thirty-five cents each and at one time I had a dozen, some of them quite small and others almost as large as standard tame mallards. But Pete, runty as he was, remained leader of the band, always at head of the procession when they waddled about the barnyard in close-order single file. Pete was not too spectacular on foot, having extremely short legs, even for a mallard, and he would frequently fall over a corncob or clump of grass, whereupon the duck behind him would fall over Pete and Pete would get up and lash out in petulant rage while the other decoys, both hens and drakes, would stretch up their necks in alarm and quack with excitement.

In the water or in the air Pete was something else. One summer the decoys stayed at another hunter's farm and there were some big Muscovy ducks there. Pete, of course, chose to challenge the supremacy of an enormous drake scaling about six times Pete's fighting weight, and came up on the short end—but that was on land. Later, when the big Muscovy took a cruise on the pond, Pete dived and attacked from below. The surface was carpeted with white feathers as the victim squawked in terror and headed for shore while Pete bobbed triumphantly, his beak full of down.

At the old railroad pond where I hunted Pete soon proved he was an escape artist of Houdini caliber. I never had real decoy collars and fastened the birds by several amateurish methods. None ever got loose except Pete, who was figuring how to get free even as he hit the water. I don't know how many times he made it but I never figured out a neck fastening that would hold him without strangling him. The first time he got loose he took off and circled the pond, just out of gun range for other hunters, one of whom tried him just for luck. After that I sadly clipped his wings. I'd always enjoyed seeing him fly around the farm.

When Pete was on the loose (which seems now to have been on most hunting days) he would horse around a little way from the tethered birds, preening his showy feathers and rolling water off his back.

When I pushed the old skiff out to pick up the other decoys

Pete would watch with apprehensive interest. Both of us knew
what was coming, for Pete was a social mallard and there was
a sure way to catch him.

I'd sack up all of the other decoys except for a single neur-
otic Susie, usually one named Repeat, whom I would tether
back in the cattails just out of the water. The cattails were
seamed with trails made by muskrats, hunters and whatnot
and Repeat would be anchored in one of those leading to open
water but curving enough to obstruct her view—and Pete's.

There would be silence for a little while with me crouched
in the cattails just off the little path and ready to dive on Pete
the moment he appeared. Then the lady duck would feel the
sudden oppression of loneliness and give forth an ear-shaking
quack followed by a series of forlorn calls interspersed with
brief pauses for an answer.

At first Pete would appear to pay no attention. He would
stand up in the water, flap his wings and go through other mo-
tions designed to express his joy at freedom, even moving a bit
farther away from shore. But after four or five minutes he
would become lonely and fidgety, edging gradually toward the
water's edge and beginning tentative calls that became more
urgent as he neared the inevitable.

Eventually Pete would come apprehensively up the little
path, his head pushed forward, his eyes rolling and his quacks
quivering with excitement. The feathers on the back of his
neck would be erect. And when he came within range I would
jump on him with my gunny sack and Pete would give a sort
of death call, half quack and half squawk, the hen would top it
off with her horrified quacking, and the excitement would be
over until the next hunt.

Although a great deal has been written about decoy placement and many artists have drawn decoy layouts I believe I
once used the ultimate. It involved a chickenwire fence and a
telescope the length of a wading staff. The fence made a pen
half in and half out of a farm pond and I could see it from my

upstairs bedroom in the old farmhouse a quarter-mile away. I kept a dozen live decoys in that pen, feeding them daily, and they could spend their time on either land or water. Each dawn I would focus my telescope on the pen and count the ducks. If there were extra birds I would approach the pen from behind the dam and stand up. The wild ones would fly but the decoys had clipped wings. Lest this be interpreted as a mass slaughter let me say that we lived far from a flight route and a duck or two a week was a good score.

I took my decoys to college, storing them in a garage that happened to be almost beneath the sleeping porch of the Phi Mu sorority house. I had small coops without bottoms and would keep two or three ducks with water and feed in each coop. The morning hunts would begin when I packed up the decoys about four a.m. on days when I had no early classes. I'd stumble into the garage, half asleep, and grab each bird by flashlight to stuff it into a sack—then off to some nearby coal-mining strip pits where Charley Osborn and I had a blind.

It was along about midway in the waterfowl season when I heard firsthand of a unique psychological problem. It was a class in English literature and just behind me were two coeds of considerable attraction.

"It's driving me out of my mind," confided one of the girls. "I know it can't be real but if it's a dream I don't know what it means. It happens about four o'clock in the morning—and I'll tell you what it sounds like." She looked about to see if anyone was listening but didn't catch me for I was facing straight forward. "It sounds like somebody catching ducks. Catching *ducks.*"

The other girl giggled but stopped short as she realized her friend was really serious. I never revealed my inside information of the sounds heard from the Phi Mu sleeping porch but it was about that time I became more interested in the girls than in duck hunting and I really can't remember what became of all those decoys.

The Skunk Trappers ➤➤➤➤➤➤➤➤➤

IT WAS HARD TO WARM THE COŔNERS of the schoolroom on those cold winter mornings so if you'd raise your hand the teacher would let you sit by the stove where there were benches but no desks. That was a happy break in routine and although little study was accomplished in such close-order seating the teacher could not refuse those who feigned the agonies of freezing.

It became chain reaction and the entire student body would crowd together on the stoveside benches while the soft coal inside turned the bowl pink. There was a sheet-iron jacket for safety and even that got pretty warm. I remember a long, vertical yellow streak on it, the result of an experiment in pressing a crayon against the hot metal. It melted and ran.

The trappers were likely to be a little late, removing their overshoes in the wooden hall with thunderous efforts, and since school would be in order or in the process of being called to order they conveyed their morning bulletins to each other in pantomime or hissing whispers. The teacher would wear a resigned look, for she guessed what was to come.

There is nothing unpleasant about the faint scent of skunk on sharp winter air and I confess to liking it in moderation. In close quarters it loses its allure swiftly.

When the trappers took their places on the stoveside benches there might be a faint trace of skunk odor and the prettiest of the girls would wrinkle her nose a little, but as the old stove did its work there would be a distinct aroma that spread and thickened, the heat working into chilled cotton sweaters and denim overalls, one or more of the trappers showing a mixture of pride and embarrassment.

The prettiest of the girls would express nausea while the second-prettiest girl and the third-prettiest girl would wrinkle their noses and those boys who had not caught skunks recently would snicker uncontrollably. If the sun was bright and the day warmed quickly the teacher would force open a sticky window and wish earnestly that she had taken a commercial course instead of "normal training."

The successful trapper or trappers might be banished to a far corner of the single room or, best of all, sent home wearing the aura of affluence. A trapped skunk meant real spending money and even the girls probably kept score.

The skunk was at the top of our trapping list and a large, prime one with very little white in his fur might bring as much as five dollars. There were price lists from the big St. Louis fur companies that listed a "black" as high as fifteen dollars, but no one I knew ever sold one for that and maybe such premium prices never were paid. A high "price list" compared with more conservative ones was likely to draw extra shipments from youthful believers but when the grading was done by the buyers even the finest pelts we could produce would fall far down the list.

The animals were classified by their stripes, listed as broad stripes, narrow stripes, short stripes and blacks. A "black," most valuable of all, would have only a little wishbone of white on its head and neck, and some of the "broads" carried almost as much white as black.

The little spotted civets brought much less and smelled about the same. Opossums were generally worth less than a dollar. Muskrats were around a dollar but not very plentiful in southeastern Kansas in those days.

Although we studied trapping literature much more carefully than arithmetic we really didn't catch much with the elaborate sets described there. Most of our fur was taken with No. 1 or 1½ Victor or Oneida traps set at holes under old farm buildings near forested creeks. Since skunks breed true to color to some extent, it was possible to find a den used by a whole family of short stripes and blacks, and my banner year resulted from such a windfall. It was under an old stone house, long abandoned as a residence and then used for grain storage, and together with the usual complement of opossums and a civet or two my winter's catch was quite impressive.

My father took no part in the sale of my furs, leaving all details to me as business training, and I drove a fairly hard bargain except for the year that the fur buyer actually rode up to the school building just as school was letting out. He'd seen my furs at our place, asked for me in a loud voice, rode a handsome horse, and so flattered me with attention before all of the other gaping kids that he bought my catch for much less than it was worth. I don't recall the price but his name was Hominy Divine. Dad shook his head but said I could sell my fur where I wanted to.

It was the trappers' supply catalogs and price lists that had us almost uncontrollable with excitement for weeks before the fur season opened on December 1. They bore the famous names of Taylor, Funsten, Fouke, Biggs and the like, and most of the fur houses were located about St. Louis, descendants and offshoots of the companies that had dealt with the mountain men of a hundred years before.

There were the prepared scents for all sorts of furbearers, imaginative artists depicting a parade of prime animals drawn inexorably to traps baited with the secret formulas. I bought some of those foul-smelling mixtures.

And each company had its own "smoker," a device for driving animals from dens. The artist showed a hunter standing at a den entrance with an overheated rifle, shooting a fortune in fur as the infallible smoker sent the animals to their death. My father said his ordinary bee smoker (used at bee trees) would be just as good. You filled a compartment with rags or other smoky combustibles and pumped a bellows. I never got any skunks or anything else that way and I secretly felt my father didn't really have the word on that.

Then there were the murderous "set guns," .22 rifles mounted to fire when an animal pulled on a bait attached to a

hooked rod. Even I could see that such a contraption would wipe out most of the neighborhood dogs before getting to the fur animals so I never got one. It was rather expensive anyway.

The gun sections were pored over most of all. They showed the standard American makes as well as imported exotics, including old military weapons and the cheapest firearms available. The Hamilton singleshot .22 was listed at $2.44 with a brass-lined barrel that was good for only a few accurate shots. After those few shots I sawed mine off and tried to make a pistol of it.

On school days we went to bed early and ran our traps at dawn but on Friday night things were different and we'd go fur hunting. Night hunting for opossum and skunks was profitable for experienced men with hounds. We were handicapped by having only farm dogs and being afraid of the dark—but we had lanterns, carbide lights and considerable spirit.

We hunted through the creek bottoms where the elms were bare, their leaves making noisy carpets. We knew of some persimmon patches and I have seen an opossum in the top of a small persimmon tree, a fat, gray ball as far up as it could get and stupidly resigned to whatever might happen with barking dogs, flickering lights and yelling kids below.

There were only two boys and a pair of dogs the night we found the skunk in the open woods a long way from any kind of a den. Joe Bennett and I heard the dogs bark, just a plain farm-dog bark and not the mellow voice of a trailing hound. They were only a little way ahead of us and when we heard them make a snarling attack and then collapse with yelps of discomfort we knew about what had happened.

I had started running with the first barks and found the dogs rolling in the leaves and pushing their noses along the ground to clear their eyes of well-aimed skunk scent. Far ahead of me my carbide light showed a black shadow hurrying away and I ran after the skunk, knowing all of those things about grabbing one by the tail and not getting stunk up. I followed fast and the carbide lamp flickered out, leaving me trying to adjust my eyes to weak moonlight. I stood stock still and then heard the skunk running on the leaves somewhere up ahead and I went on to overtake the undulating, furry blob. I reached for it but it eluded me and then I dived on it like a halfback after a fumble, for clothes can be soaked in vinegar or even thrown away and a short-stripe skunk is worth money.

The Word Is "Whoa!"➤➤➤➤➤➤➤

KELLY, THE WORLDLY-WISE BRITTANY, was backing Murphy's point but he had the look of a small boy lying in wait with a snowball. Kelly was rolling his eyes, turning his head a little to look at me, twitching his tail involuntarily, and if dogs can giggle, Kelly was giggling.

Murphy, all fifty-five-pound English pointer of him, was rigid in a picture point which made bedraggled little Kelly look shabby indeed standing back a respectful distance with cockleburs matted in his brindle hair and wet mud up to his belly. I hurried up as fast as I could with half-frozen mud weighting my boots. It was a place for Hungarian partridge all right, a strand of dead weeds next to a Western irrigation ditch, yet there was something about Kelly's attitude that made me hurry.

But I was too late and I still think Kelly said something in dog talk to Murphy because Murphy broke his point and lunged forward. Then came the surprised yelps I had feared and Murphy emerged looking like an overgrown wirehaired terrier with porcupine quills sticking in all directions from his face.

Here I was, I thought, with two dogs disabled by quills and miles from the truck, but I should have known better. Although Kelly had appeared to take enthusiastic part in the charge he was now sitting fifty yards away, quill-less as always, grinning with his tongue lolled out and evidently anticipating the fun of my yanking eighty quills out of Murphy. He had never cared much for Murphy, who was fast on his feet but not noted for being mentally swift.

I am pretty good at taking quills out of dogs as I have had considerable practice. Do it fast with good pliers and it isn't nearly as bad as it looks. I served my internship at a black-

172

powder rifle shoot years ago when a geologist's dachshund named Oiler caught a roundhouse swing from a porky's tail. Everyone else was a little slow to get with it and I figured this would be better than learning on my own dog, so I grabbed some pliers and gave instructions to the holders. I hope Oiler's owner doesn't read this but it went pretty well. Oiler tried to bite me at first but finally decided I was on his side. That was the first year I ran a bird dog in porky country and I had more practice before the year was over.

Now McGillicuddy, the thinkingest Brittany I know, still has irresistible curiosity and used to get quilled regularly, after which he'd come in and wait for the pliers. Just couldn't leave porcupines alone. There was once when he got a minor dose of quills just as a day's hunt started and his owner, Ben Williams, and I got him squared away and back to hunting. We hunted all day and then came back by the bushes where McGillie had got it early that morning. You guessed it. He went back in there and came out with a faceful, wearing the look of an addict who needs help.

McGillie has been bitten by rattlesnakes twice but always around his short snout and the veterinarians say he pulls back fast enough that he doesn't get a full dose of venom. He doesn't want to bite any rattlesnakes—just check them out.

Kelly never collected a quill in seven years of hunting porky country, but he liked to start each season off by getting nailed by a skunk. After opening day of the third season my wife Debie was at the garage with a jug of vinegar before I could get Kelly unloaded.

"I smelled the truck when it came into the drive," she said.

Then when old Kelly began to get skunk savvy he acquired a sense of humor about it. One day he made some funny points around an old wagon wreck out in the grass country. I went over and kicked the junk and a skunk cut loose at me. I looked around to find Kelly sitting a hundred feet away with his ears up, his tongue out on one side and with that giggly look.

Having seen dogs get into trouble pretty frequently I conclude that "Whoa!" is the most important command in the trainer's manual. Kelly knew it well but he'd ignore it now and then, like the time he found a big badger out in the open. The badger, who was quite capable of busting one of Kelly's legs, or possibly killing him, was making badger fight noises and feeling for a soft place on the ground just in case he had to dig in. I told Kelly whoa, but Kelly had to have some fun so he got back quite a distance and ran at the badger full tilt, went over him and nipped him on the way. It happened pretty fast and I've never seen a badger so mad. He blew froth and sounded like a clothes dryer full of bobcats. Kelly never went near him again, just sat down fifty yards away and giggled.

But "Whoa!" is a pretty important command.

‹‹‹‹‹‹‹‹‹‹‹‹‹‹‹‹‹‹‹‹‹‹‹‹‹‹‹‹‹Waders

SOME OF MY ASSOCIATES CONSIDER IT very droll of me that I fill a bathtub and sit down in it every time I get a new pair of waders. Most of them are trusting types who figure no waders could ever leak.

One of these believers recently traveled two thousand miles by air, car and boat only to find that the cold water came up on the inside of his new waders at the same rate it climbed on the outside. Better he should have gotten wet in the bathtub the way I have a couple of times.

I don't know anything about the procedures of building waders but I am sure that many of the post-manufacture inspections are carried out under very dry conditions. I still feel that for fifty or sixty bucks new waders shouldn't leak much.

As the years go by most ardent trout fishermen will find that they have invested more in their waders than in their Payne rods or their Hardy reels. In addition to keeping out the water, waders are intended to prevent slipping on slick rocks, and some of the devices for this are wondrous to behold, ranging from felt (which for some reason costs more than Oriental tapestry) to soft iron hobs and an assortment of spikes, aluminum plates and secret concoctions of metal and glue.

Each has a particular kind of slick bottom for which it is particularly suited. I had my long, sharp spike period and did very well on my first day's fishing with them until I started to cross a wooden footbridge and became stuck somewhere near the middle, the spikes having penetrated the wood and refused to let go. I pulled myself loose with the handrail and decided the spikes were too long.

Many years ago someone announced a gooey solution that you smeared on your wader soles and then added Carborundum chips. Please do not consider my experience with it in

the light of later developments as I think it was first introduced before the boys in the lab had finished their experiments.

I first tried it when the Madison River bottom was so slippery I suspect the stonefly nymphs were using cleats. I meticulously followed the complex directions of heating, smearing, drying and Carborundum-chip sprinkling, the whole process taking several sessions and considerable time, my wife looking up now and then from her fly-tying and admiring my work.

When I reached the river I was amazed at my surefootedness and even did a little pirouette atop a mossy boulder a foot under the surface. I also discarded my collapsible wading staff, which had shown a tendency to collapse easily when I leaned on it and with great difficulty when I tried to put it in the car trunk.

I waded deeper and deeper into the noisy and slanting Madison, my confident feet showing less and less concern for their placement, and I hooked a two-pound brown trout that came up for a Sofa Pillow fly.

There was a split in the river at that point and the resultant island was bordered by perfect trout water, heretofore untouched by craven anglers with ordinary waders, so why not cross the run and work from the other side? This I did with a certain flair, attracting the frank admiration of a great blue heron who'd had the island to himself up until then.

About the island I really didn't need my faultless footing, for the water ran easier. For two hours I fished my private preserve and I caught several trout. It was almost dusk when I decided to recross the split but when I first waded into faster water it seemed I slipped a little. Possibly my imagination. But I slipped again and went back to the island shore to see what was wrong. My damned Carborundum chips had worn off and my soles were almost as smooth as the rocks they were supposed to stick to. Like Icarus, who did a Brodie when the wax of his jury-rigged wings melted near the sun, I had lost my edge over the elements.

So I looked up and down the river, not for help but to be sure no one was watching, and I walked until the Madison upset me and then swam a little. The Madison is fed largely by melting snow. I was on the other shore before I remembered I had a Leica in the back of my fishing vest.

‹‹‹‹‹‹‹‹‹‹‹ Theory of Relativity

I HAVE THIS THEORY OF RELATIVITY about hunting and fishing and if you don't thoroughly understand it you might sum it up as meaning the more you get the more you want. That isn't the idea at all.

Like everybody else I wish I was rich, but I'm afraid that would take a lot of fun out of life in some areas. For example, if I could afford a yacht I doubt if I'd really appreciate a new bass boat with an electric motor. To buy the bass boat I had to put an extra twenty-five thousand miles on our Ford, which had shown signs of not really wanting to go another twenty-five thousand miles. This made the bass boat considerably more valuable, the same way duck shooting can be more fun if you really should be working.

But the best illustration of my theory concerns .22 short rifle cartridges. There was a time in my life when I had no ambition at all further than owning all the .22 shorts I could shoot in my Stevens Crackshot rifle. Now that was about 1923 and you could get a box of shorts for twenty-nine cents. At one time I had a full box of fifty plus nine other cartridges I had traded marbles for.

My folks were glad to furnish a modest number of cartridges for serious hunting but idle expenditure of them for target practice was unacceptable. At the time it never occurred to me that I would ever be able to shoot all of them I wanted and not really give a damn about it. When that time came (you don't have to be a tycoon to own a few cartons of .22s) I took a lever-action Model 39 Marlin I'd just bought, and did quite a bit of shooting. It was fun all right and I'd still enjoy it, but after I had plinked a hundred supine bean cans and pulverized several hundred Osage oranges thrown into the air (with an appropriate number of misses) it occurred to me that I was

thinking more and more about a custom-stocked Winchester
.30–06 and some handloading tools.

I have some friends who lost sleep and promotions in order
to go hunting and fishing through most of their active lives.
Then they got their gold watches from the company, moved to
waterfront retirement cottages with their boats tied at the
back door—and quit hunting and fishing because it was too
easy. Most of them haven't figured it out but the inconve-
nience and effort is much of the fun.

Now a few million dollars don't necessarily take the fun out
of going hunting but sometimes they can. There was this man
I knew who left the business to his hired hands while he went
hunting, and since he hadn't managed to do it before he decided to skip the rabbit and squirrel preliminaries and go off
to Africa and do it right—sort of get it out of the way with one
move, so to speak.

When he came back with his trophies and the movies he'd
taken I was really anxious to hear about the trip. He said the
highlight of his expedition was a lion he'd potted from a truck.
Even in those days using a truck as a lion blind (motor running) was perhaps a mite beyond the law but any African lion
with a full mane is worthy of mention and I pressed him for
details.

It seems he had offended the lion by shooting him a little
and the lion had come over and cuffed the truck about considerably before members of the party managed to do him in and
take the truck to a body shop. I wondered what kind of bullet
had irritated the lion but the hunter didn't know about that.
He didn't know what kind of rifle he had used but he thought
it was made in Europe with lions in mind. The thought of a
man going hunting without knowing what kind of gun he had,
and without the advance pleasure of buying it after thumbing
a batch of catalogs and specifications, and without giving up
anything to get it, was beyond my experience. He hadn't even
waited for squirrels when he was a kid, pretending they were
leopards, but when he got back to the office maybe he had a

sense of accomplishment and he had the hunting business taken care of. It was a little like making a touchdown after the other team had gone home. Maybe he should have had the truck mounted.

It takes a lot of trouble to make a good hunt. A long time ago I sat in a scraggly cattail blind in the Midwest and watched the high mallards and pintails bore south through snow and a little sleet. None of them looked at my decoys as far as I could tell, and it seemed they must have come a very long way with a long way to go. It was cold enough that there was quite a bit of ice around the pond's edges and one of my hip boots leaked just a little. I'd been up since three a.m. and I had to be at school at nine. My dry runs at getting off the forefinger safety of my old Model 12 Winchester hadn't worked out very well for the past few minutes as my hands were pretty cold. The only way I could move it was with my thumb and then I couldn't bend my forefinger around the trigger in the unlikely case that one of those hurrying flocks with wind on their tails should dive down into my half-dozen decoys. I planned to use my middle finger.

When I picked up, shipping a quart of ice water in the boot that didn't leak, I dreamed of hunting ducks where the flights start, somewhere up in Canada, or at least north of Kansas City, which was as far that way as I'd been. I thought about it while I nursed the Model T back to the main road and the manifold heater began putting out heavenly, smelly heat.

Thirty-five years later I just happened to be where the flights start at the time they begin. There I was in the pothole country of Alberta and I hadn't even been thinking about ducks. It was a wonderful sharptail-grouse shooting trip, the dog had pointed and retrieved, the rosebushes were a dull red on the hills, and two of us were smug with success and comfort in our camper.

Then I remembered the scraggly blind and the storm-driven flocks and I began to notice the bunches of ducks that seemed to be forever dropping into a little grass pond half a mile away. No one was gunning them, duck season was open, and it appeared I could approach the pond from a shallow draw, so I dug out some duck loads, found a camouflaged jacket, and began the sneak. It was easy and I didn't even stoop until the last few yards. In a preliminary peek I had seen two glossy mallard drakes near where I would come on range and when I stepped into sight they went straight up. I got both of them, a triumph of marksmanship for me, and barely heard the roar of wings that came out of the pond grass and weeds behind them where a hundred unseen birds had jumped. My partner released the dog from the camper and he charged into the water. There were three other dead birds I'd dropped incidentally as they rose behind my two drakes, and a dozen more kept trying to come in while I fussed with the dog.

They were young pintails and mallards with a long trip ahead of them. It was too easy and I guess it had been more fun in the cattail blind with no shots at all. You have to work at it.

<<<<<<<<<<<<<<<<<<<<< Old Empties

Early in the evening a mule deer isn't likely to be in the center of a mountain clearing. He appears first at the edge and I never know how long he has been there. I may have had my glasses on that spot a dozen times, looking for his blocky gray outline or the movement of his lighter-colored legs, but when I finally find him he shows plainly and suddenly, and I wonder if I have missed him the last time I looked.

He is likely to be at the edge of any one of half a dozen parks I can watch from some high ridge, often an overlook so logical that it has been used by generations of hunters, and perhaps there are flint chips left a thousand years ago by a bowman who shaped an arrow point as he watched the lower slopes.

I climbed to such an overlook in Montana's Crazy Mountains, going slowly through the lower stand of timber, watchful of small openings where a deer might stop to study whatever had moved him from his bed, and keeping my eye on a bouldered and rimrocked section of the high spine, sure that I could see a great swatch of game country once I got there. When I paused to rest I stood with one foot a little uphill and with my rifle butt on the slope and I shifted the little rucksack with its store of emergency things, but I kept my eyes on the high ridge most of the time as if constant inspection might bring it nearer.

Once I reached the ridge peak, moving so that I would be among giant stones rather than emerging as a stark silhouette, I glanced backward to be sure of my twilight route to camp, and then sat down on a boulder that was almost against a larger rock—a natural rest for a deer or elk hunter's .270 and equally good for a mountain man's muzzleloader. A raven passed above me, twisting his head in curiosity, and I heard

the wind through shaggy breast feathers and wingtips as he sideslipped a little and then wheeled off down the slope with one noncommittal croak.

I felt the ghostly presence of hunters long gone, men who might have worn beartooth necklaces or buckskin and carried spears or flintlocks, and they seemed to admire my compact binoculars and telescopic sight, but perhaps they felt my lugged boots were too noisy. Just below the ridge peak was a trail with the round-toed track of an elk and the heart-shaped marks of deer, but I saw no game that day except a muley doe and her two fawns of the year, far across a canyon, dipping their noses into the bushes between casual looks about. On the north side of my bench-rest boulder was a little patch of snow left from an early fall storm and there was a single coyote's track at the edge of it, for such a lookout is not likely to be missed by any little wolf in the vicinity.

Then I looked at the fist-sized stones nearer my feet and saw something that did not quite fit but had taken on their color and had settled between two of them, invisible except from almost directly above. It was an empty .44–40 case, that old frontier favorite that worked in both rifles and revolvers and killed more game than any other cartridge, and it seemed that the ghosts of all the old hunters grinned when I found it. I tossed the old brass back among the loose rocks that had been churned up when the mountains were made and I suppose it is still there, although I am sure a younger hunter has since climbed to the ridge and sat on the rock with the natural bench rest beside it.

We should pick up our empties now but it was only recently that they became plentiful enough to be called litter and they have somehow been a part of game country, eerily predictible in those logical spots where a hunter could expect a shot, and somehow encouraging when game is lacking if they are not too recent.

In Alaska I climbed for hours to a wind-ripped mountain top for rock ptarmigan, braced my feet against the torrent of air that would have shredded any but ground-hugging vegetation, and watched the first birds of the hunt as they dived down the slope and out of sight beyond a precipice. As I ejected a wasted empty and then decided to pick it up I saw a scrap of brass, the head of an old 12-gauge paper shell, the paper long gone, and I have no idea how many generations of ptarmigan have flushed from that tiny fold in the mountain and dived over that windy precipice.

There were several years when I did not look for mallards along a Western creek I used to know well. When I went back last year there were new willows and some rosebushes I didn't remember but the muskrats were busy as before and a white-tail deer showed a flag briefly as I slipped through the cottonwoods.

I heard a single soft quack that gave away the flock of mallards in the little slough ahead and I tried to recall the best approach, finally deciding upon a little patch of brush on the high bank. I inched to it on hands and knees and then stood up suddenly, my gun muzzles probing a little uncertainly, the gun half mounted before I could find the birds. They slapped the water hard with their wings and most of them went through the trees so that I could not get a decent shot, but one big curly-tailed drake powered straight up into open sky where I killed him as he began a turn, and he came down with a thump at the edge of the slough, his orange legs hardly moving.

Bright-red plastic shotgun shells seem to last forever, despite storm, sun and flood, and add little to a pastoral scene, so I stooped to pick up the empty I had ejected. Beside the fresh one were two others, still red but dulled by the weather—the ones I had left there years before when other mallards had towered from the little slough. So I stared at them and mused upon the things that had happened to me and the places I had been since that other fall.

Don't litter. Pick up your empties.

‹‹‹‹‹‹‹‹‹ A Dog For the West

I HEARD FROM MURPHY THE OTHER NIGHT. He'd been gone for quite a while and it was nice to learn he'd found work. Murphy is a big lemon-and-white pointer with a square head and polka-dot ears. He and I were associated for some time but our arrangement didn't work out.

In the West, English pointers are pretty scarce. There they go stronger for shorthairs, Brittanies, and some of the other "foreign" breeds. A while back I got into a discussion about bird dogs, and in order to show I was a loyal Southerner I told a gathering of Westerners that one big-going English pointer could find more birds than a whole kennelful of those other mutts.

After that, there was a pregnant silence, as the novelists say, and I knew that either I or a glass of bourbon had overdone it. But it was too late.

One of my outraged listeners wrote a letter to Dave Duffey, who writes about dogs for *Outdoor Life*. Duffey, who I thought was a friend, finked out on me, saying I didn't know pointers from poodles—or something like that.

This put it squarely up to the pointers, so I got me a big long-legged pup named Murphy who came from field-trial stock. This, I said, would show them how Hungarian partridge should be hunted.

I had wanted a wide-ranger and that's what I got. If you had paid attention you might have seen Murphy passing your house on one of his wider casts. After Murphy found there were no strings on the whistle he abandoned his practice of coming to it and adopted the system of running until he was lost and then howling for me. Although he sometimes pointed rigidly, the birds would have paired off and started nesting by the time I could get there. When I found him he would take

the attitude that *I* had been lost and would take off again without letting me get too close. As I look back, I realize he generally came in at feeding time whether lost or not.

I took him to a dog trainer but the trainer used a system Murphy didn't approve of so he dismantled the kennel and left. It never occurred to him to come home but a fellow found him and mistakenly thought he was doing me a favor by bringing him to me. I had absentmindedly left my own name on his collar plate.

He was mild-mannered about everything but his hunting, and it was embarrassing to see somebody's thirty-pound Brittany kick the stuffing out of him for exercise. When Murphy got his mouth full of porcupine quills he'd simply stand like a Christian martyr and let me pull them out. I admired this quality but wondered why he confused porcupines with doggie bones.

Finally, I had had it up to the shell vest with Murphy and gave him to a trainer who dealt in field-trial dogs. I gave him to the trainer when the trainer was not at home, slipping him into the kennel as if he were a time bomb. I stuck his registration papers on the door with a porcupine quill.

The other night I got a telephone call from a hunter friend in the Rockies. He wanted to know if I remembered Murphy, which was a silly question and like asking me if I remembered World War II. He said he had news of Murphy. I winced a little at that because news of Murphy had always been on a par with news of the Boston strangler.

Murphy, he said, had lost a field trial. It seems some champ from the South had beaten him with Murph coming in a tight second. But that was all right, he guessed, because it was the first one Murph had lost.

The Wallfish ➤➤➤➤➤➤➤➤➤➤➤➤➤➤

IT HAD BEEN GOING ON a long time before I even heard of it. It was started by two Eastern trout fishermen, Dan Bailey and his long-time friend John MacDonald. The idea was simply to outline a large trout on a wall, or on a board to be hung on the wall, so that the fish's true form and dimensions would not be forgotten and comrades not present when the fish was caught might view its image with admiration or envy at later dates.

I must tell of how the "wallfish" became one word, spoken as if it were a separate species, although this tale is not of the wallfish itself so much as it is an account of how the thing became a sort of albatross about my neck, or possibly an albatross in absentia since my troubles sprang from having no wallfish. Untold pages have been written about Dan Bailey's Wall of Fame, a sort of anglers' holy place that became a tourist attraction, an advertising stroke of genius, and a status symbol to a scale that almost frightened Dan Bailey.

Dan Bailey went west a long time ago to fish for trout, not just a casual trip but an uprooting and replanting, because the West had the best trout fishing and Dan went there, hopefully to spend his life where the trout fishing was better than in his beloved Eastern brooks. He and his wife Helen found the cold, quick streams of Yellowstone Park, some of them joining together to rush through Yankee Jim Canyon and on through Paradise Valley as the powerful Yellowstone, and by the Yellowstone the Baileys stayed. Dan tied his immaculate trout flies in a tent at one time, and when he had opened his small shop in Livingston, Montana, he knew that, come hell or an overflow of the Yellowstone, he was a college professor no longer. He would live with the trout and sell his flies.

Some time along the way he transplanted this Eastern business of the wall fish. It was two words then. He came up with the weight of four pounds as the minimum. Catch a fish of four pounds or more on a fly and he would outline it on a plaque and put it on his wall. Later, it became necessary to submit a larger fish if it came from a lake. There came a time when painting up the wall fish each winter was quite a task, supervised by Red Monical, Dan's younger partner, and they were made from outlines kept on heavy paper and filed during the busy summer and fall season.

When I first visited Bailey's, the walls were well crowded with the trout outlines and the business was growing wildly, to Dan's seeming perplexity. There was a long bench of lady fly-tiers and already Dan was spending much of his time typing letters to fly fishermen all over the world, answers to queries about flies, guides and Western fishing. There is a tendency to treasure those letters. Already, Bailey's was a gathering point for dozens of regulars who had found themselves coming every year.

On our first trip Bailey's was just another stop for fishing information, and we found it heading a list of Western stopoffs given us by Joe Brooks, whose grave now looks down on Paradise Valley. There had been a heavy snow runoff from the high country that year and the Yellowstone was muddy, so Dan directed us to other areas. We had good fishing and when we came back I reported our success to Dan across a counter in the fly shop. He hung on every word until he had the essential information, and then, although he continued to look pleasantly at me, he clicked me off almost audibly when I began to babble things that were really stories of fishing adventure rather than fishing facts—and just as it dawned on me that Dan Bailey had heard multiple thousands of fishing stories and I paused foolishly, Dan said, without moving or taking his eyes off me:

"I know now where that thirty-six cents went, Red."

And his partner, Red Monical, spoke up from somewhere back in the bookkeeping end to say wait a minute, he'd get the record and check. After the thirty-six cents had been ac-

counted for in writing, Dan began telling of new places for me
to fish.

Dan Bailey does not look like Dan Bailey at all at first
glance. The name is the one he was born with and is accidentally the perfect one for a sporting-goods dealer, whereas
other outdoorsy names have been selected deliberately by
businessmen wishing to sell safari jackets or sleeping bags.
Dan's name sounds big and breezy, but at first glance Dan is
small and unassuming and you look the second time to see that
he has a boxer's build, even to the taut midsection and very
slightly muscle-rounded shoulders. His backcast goes high and
smooth and he goes endlessly in the mountains when he takes
his rifle for deer. In his sixties he danced confidently on tiptoe
to keep icy water from his waders as he worked to the perfect
spot for his deft flies.

But this is not primarily about Dan Bailey or the fly shop
that has spread in all directions until it is hard to recall the individual growth steps it has taken. This is about the wallfish,
and if the shop had not grown immensely, it would have been
necessary to keep the wallfish plaques in some sort of giant file
so that last year's wallfisherman could see his fish on demand.
As it is, the new walls accommodate the banks of wooden
trout, grouped as to sizes, and it is a happy angler who is introduced to a stranger in Houston or Detroit and is told immediately that the new acquaintance has seen his fish on Dan
Bailey's wall.

But although this is a pleasant thing and now has become
traditional, there was a time when I would gladly have burned
those wooden trout before the Park County courthouse and I
might have thrown the ashes at Dan Bailey without even telling him why.

Probably it was the salmon-fly hatch that really tied us to
Montana. Debie and I caught it just right on the Madison
River over near Ennis on our first Montana fishing visit. The
"salmon flies" are really big stone flies, and during their hatch
they lumber about over the Madison and other rivers, emerg-

ing in such volume that the streamside willows often bend
with their awkward weight and the big nymphal shucks last
for months along the shores, some of them still clinging to
branches or stones and others easily found at the water's edge,
sometimes in little windrows where current has piled them.

It can be a sort of outsized dry-fly fishing, and until then I
had thought little of dry-fly trout over two pounds, but everything was bigger now—the flies, the heavier rod, the wider,
swifter river and the blurred reddish-brown rise of big "lochs"
far out where the hurrying current distorted the patchwork of
varicolored bottom stones. And although most of the dry-fly
delicacy was absent, there was the glug of big rising fish, sometimes clearly audible over the unbroken roar of the river.

At first Debie tied her special flies in our cabin at Bud
Baker's Riverside Motel at Ennis, merely taking the pattern of
Dan Bailey's faultless Sofa Pillows and adding more hackle to
the bushy squirrel hair so that the finished product floated
high and grotesque in spite of the froth and fury of the current
that quickly drowned smaller things. We innocently called
her work the Haystack Fly, not knowing that the name was a
plagarism of some other Haystack of some other place.

The Madison was a little high and especially slick that year
and our feet hurt from fitting felt soles to rounded boulders.
When the sun was hot we sometimes waded wet in blue jeans,
often shivering through a cloudy period or a chilly shower,
and we caught many three-pound trout and some within scant
ounces of four pounds. At first we did not weigh them and Dan
Bailey's wall was only a part of Montana like the furious July 4
rodeo at Ennis and the white dots of sheepherders' arks on the
high pastures.

Then we thought it would be good to take four-pound trout
to Dan Bailey's place and join the angling immortals on his
wall, and I gradually realized that four pounds is not exactly a
random figure where trout are concerned. A three-pound,
fourteen-ounce trout is a fine catch but not exactly unusual in
the Madison or Yellowstone valleys, and for some perverse

reason of nature not many fish acquire those other two ounces.

We temporarily abandoned the Riverside Motel and camped on the Madison's bank that year; I recall Debie cooking over an open fire in waders and raingear while sleet and cold rain hissed into her wavering little sprig of flame. We were younger then.

We learned that the salmon-fly hatch moves progressively farther upstream and that sometimes the wake of the spree is better than the time when the natural flies are thick on the water, turning helplessly in the current and so plentiful that there could never be enough fish to take them all. Once they have acquired the taste for salmon flies and the winged ones are no longer there in quantity, the big fish are likely to be looking eagerly upward at your imitation before they finally decide to go back to the underwater forage that makes up the majority of their diet in normal times. But though we caught and released dozens of good fish we caught no four-pounders during the hatch or immediately after it, and it was weeks later that we returned to the Madison to fish Muddler Minnow streamers, generally floating them at first and then pulling them under for a retrieve instead of picking them up like dry flies.

It was not like the stone-fly hatch, when brown trout, rainbows, cutthroats and big whitefish showed their colors in an unmistakable shimmer as they came up for dry flies, but there were good fish to be had, and when I hooked the big brown far out near a boulder I found myself guessing his size, my first inkling that the wallfish sickness was upon me.

The fish jumped once, the leader sagging behind him as he took line upstream, then swung down and across to nose down behind a rock and send sullen tugs up the line as good trout are likely to do. When I moved him from that rock he went to another and finally he dropped downstream, a clumsy, nearly dead weight, and I waded gingerly to shore, knowing that piece of river well, and working him into nearly dead water against the willows where several boulders had fenced away the current. There I got him into six inches of depth, where he wrapped up in the leader and finally rolled over on his side to be scooped up, and the pocket scales showed exactly four pounds. Then I said we should go to more accurate scales, and Debie, whose mind was not yet warped to the wooden fish on the Wall of Fame, was startled. Fishing competition had never before touched our lives.

We took the trout to a shop at Ennis and the proprietor wrote a testimony that it had, in fact, weighed four pounds exactly, but I saw that the scales actually showed three pounds, fifteen and one-half ounces.

"I made it four pounds because it's undoubtedly dried out more than an ounce," the man said.

I nodded but there was a taste of ashes. We went back to our fishing and we ate the big trout.

It was the next year that Debie caught her wallfish in the Yellowstone, casting a streamer fly in a favorite pool of ours. Even in those days, less than twenty years ago, it was very rare to find another fisherman in a favorite pool, and we have fished that one many times without seeing another soul, either there or during the short walk through the cottonwoods, past the cattle pens, across the creek and downstream to where a heavy rapids bends into the long, straight pool with its rocky bar. The mallards loaf on the bar in fall and when the season wears on there will often be two or three green-winged teal that sizzle from nowhere, plop into the shallow little pool between the bar and the earth bank, stare in what appears to be horror when they see a fisherman, and zip off to somewhere else.

Fall is really the time for wallfish, and more and more fishermen have found that the big brown trout, preparing for spawning, like long streamers in fall. Most of these anglers have used smaller flies and lighter rods during the summer in the West or elsewhere, but as the first frosts appear they think of big fish and heavier tackle and their methods would work for steelhead. In recent years they have used sinking fly lines, but that hadn't started when Debie caught her wallfish. She hooked it just before dusk and brought it around to the long, rocky bar as she has done many other fine fish, and when we decided it must be nearly a wallfish we used pocket scales, saw it was a shade over the four-pound mark, and arrived at Dan Bailey's home in darkness. He had a special scale there for just such emergencies.

It was late but Dan was not yet home from the store, so it was Helen Bailey who produced the emergency scales and the needle swung triumphantly to four pounds and one ounce— but so that Dan could see it, we left the fish and the scales in the kitchen. Then he came home and admired the fish, sat there grinning with a drink in his hand, and apologized for being late. It seems the fish tank had broken again.

The fish tank had been an essential scourge of the store for years and at that time they had not worked out a construction that would last. The glass tank was mounted in the fly-shop window and always contained a large living fish or two for display purposes. At times it seeped delicately and sent a little trickle along under the fly-tiers' bench, and on other occasions it gave way suddenly in a deluge of many gallons of water, broken glass and flopping trout. And on the evening Debie caught her wallfish the tank had broken outward into the street—but Dan hastened to explain he had, as on other occasions, rushed the disenfranchised trout to the river in time, only a few blocks away.

He looked happily at Debie's wallfish again and added as an afterthought that a man had been standing on the sidewalk looking at the fish when the big tank had given way. It seems the man had been surprised at the occurrence, Dan said, and I would consider that understatement.

"But he was all right," Dan added. "I took him into the store and dried him off."

He sipped at his drink and asked more questions about Debie's wallfish. Some of the exciting quality of Dan Bailey's store has gone since they learned how to make the fish tanks hold.

It dawned on us some time later that Debie's trout was the first woman's four-pounder to reach the wall from a stream and we treasured this milestone, but there was a change in the attitude of other fishermen where I was concerned. At first there was the kidding the husband of any fisherwoman learns to take, generally with carefully concealed pride, but then came something else—a guarded attitude that such a situation was a bit delicate and should be discussed with pointed diplomacy or carefully avoided.

Unused to being a marked man with no wallfish and married to a woman who had caught one, I began to detect a little serious sympathy being expressed cautiously by anglers who drank coffee in the Murray Hotel two doors from Bailey's. The fact that far better anglers than I had not caught wallfish was unimportant. The point is that they did not have wives who had caught wallfish, and I suspect that many of my friends felt Debie belabored me with her wooden trout at the time of any slight family disagreement.

After that first year I had relaxed about wallfish, confident that they came in time if you continued fishing with your backcast up, and I was willing to wait for mine. But after Debie caught hers I saw the thing was not that simple, and the fact I had caught a dozen or so fish of more than three pounds, twelve ounces, did not count. They were not wallfish. Each of these smaller ones was regarded by my friends as a saddening event, as if it were further proof that I could not catch a wallfish, and they told me that I could fish well enough to do it— that I was just unlucky. This, of course, made me mad as hell.

As I look back I must have been reading all sorts of things into all wellwishing, but they really got to me when they knew I was going fishing and told me they hoped I'd get the big one this time. I believe it was the third year when someone actually put his hand on my shoulder and said he felt sure

I'd get a big one that season. I would get this kind of reas-
surances, even when I started for a creek where no one suspected there was any trout of more than twelve inches.

There was the time when I went out on the Yellowstone
with Dr. A. M. McCarthy, a fine angler who has been making
the Western trip for years. I took Mac to a place where I had
broken off a big fish through awkwardness a day or two before
and we stood in heavy water and cast big streamers to a deep
pool. Within a few minutes Mac had expertly landed a fish
well over the wallfish requirement and sat down to con-
template it. Then he told me truthfully that he was sorry he
had caught it when he really didn't need another wallfish and
I needed one so badly. After that, the whole thing pushed at
me as something that had to be done, and I told Debie it was
under my skin. We were putting waterproofing on a wall tent
at the time and she said firmly that if that was how I felt about
it I might as well forego other kinds of fishing, take a big rod
and a big streamer and make a wallfish campaign. Then I felt
better and determined to follow all big fish tips. That was the
fall when the Missouri bulged with big fish up at Beaver Creek
near Helena, and that is where we went.

The big fish came up the Missouri from a downstream im-
poundment that fall, and they must have considered the
mouth of little Beaver Creek and its gravel as a spawning
area. They were brown trout and evening was the best time,
with heavy splashes out in the deep current and now and then
a big fish jumping free, usually at dusk. You might catch a big
one at any time, but when the mountain shadows came to the
river you checked your tippet and your streamer and waded a
little farther into the pressing current with the gravel shifting
a little underfoot. You cast as far as you could, the line roping
out toward the river's center and the streamer swinging
around to hurry for a space and then hang below you.

The fish were there and ready to strike, and when I felt the
five-pounder I was almost sure Dan Bailey's wall would no
longer haunt me. So I worked him to where little Beaver

Creek trickled in, unheard beside the big river's mutter, and beached him as if he were a twenty-pound steelhead while Debie stood watching, tensely silent, and too pleased and relieved to give me her usual laughing congratulations.

And once the fish was landed things were uncomplicated and I caught another wallfish and another even bigger so that the first one never made the wall at all. Debie caught some too and I was just another fisherman who came to Dan Bailey's every year instead of the marked man whose wife had a wallfish.

But the part I remember best is Mac telling me he was sorry he had caught that big trout in the Yellowstone, for now that I have had a wallfish for all these years I know it was a very nice thing to say.